PLAY AND CREATIVITY IN ART TEACHING

In *Play and Creativity in Art Teaching*, esteemed art educator George Szekely draws on his two classic volumes, *Encouraging Creativity in Art Lessons* and *From Play to Art*, to create a new book for new times. The central premise is that art teachers are not only a source of knowledge about art but also a catalyst for creating conditions that encourage students to use their own ideas for making art. By observing children at play and using props and situations familiar to them, teachers can build on children's energy and self-initiated discoveries to inspire school art that comes from the child's imagination. The foundation of this teaching approach is the belief that the essential goal of art teaching is to inspire children to behave like artists, that art comes from within themselves and not from the art teacher.

Play and Creativity in Art Teaching offers plans for the study of children's play and for discovering creative art teaching as a way to bring play into the art room. While it does not offer a teaching formula or a single set of techniques to be followed, it demystifies art and shows how teachers can help children find art in familiar and ordinary places, accessible to everyone. This book also speaks to parents and the important roles they can play in supporting school art programs and nourishing the creativity of their children.

George Szekely is Professor and Director of Graduate Studies in Art Education, University of Kentucky and is currently President-Elect of the National Art Education Association for a six-year term beginning May 2015. He was named a National Treasure by the National Art Education Association and presented with the honor of becoming a Distinguished Fellow. For his lifetime contributions to art education, he received the Victor Lowenfeld Prize and the Emanuel Barkan Award.

"George Szekely is simply a master at this topic – unparalleled in the field of art education. Play is a refreshing topic – so important in child developmental theory as described by Vygotsky and Piaget – that such a text could very well promote a dialogue about the destructive qualities of policies that emphasize 'drill and kill.' This book could easily reignite a dialogue in both the field of art education and general education about the value of imagination."

R. Barry Shauck, Boston University, USA

"George Szekely offers a unique and useful guide to explore connections between play and art making, encouraging teachers to get in touch with themselves as artists and apply what they know about play through art as teachers."

Rikki Asher, Queens College, City University of New York, USA

"Play and Creativity in Art Teaching is all about implementing Picasso's well known statement: 'Every child is an artist. The problem is how to remain an artist once we grow up.' Whereas Picasso merely hints at a direction, George Szekely draws us a detailed map we can use to guide young artists to meaningful life-sustaining Art."

Frank Asch, children's book author and illustrator

"Come sit on the floor with George Szekely—a teacher of teachers, an enthusiastic student of children's art, and a great mentor to all who would keep the joy of play in their lives. This delightful book brings together his best thoughts for parents and teachers to support play, learning, and creativity for their children and students."

Katherine Douglas, co-founder of Teaching for Artistic Behavior (TAB) and art teacher of 37 years

PLAY AND CREATIVITY IN ART TEACHING

George Szekely

Routledge
Taylor & Francis Group

NEW YORK AND LONDON

First published 2015
by Routledge
711 Third Avenue, New York, NY 10017

and by Routledge
2 Park Square, Milton Park, Abingdon, Oxon OX14 4RN

Routledge is an imprint of the Taylor & Francis Group, an informa business

© 2015 Taylor & Francis

Library of Congress Cataloging-in-Publication Data

A catalog record for this book has been requested.

ISBN: 978-0-415-66252-9 (hbk)
ISBN: 978-0-415-66253-6 (pbk)
ISBN: 978-0-203-07220-2 (ebk)

Typeset in ApexBembo
by Apex CoVantage, LLC

My creative teaching life began when I first crawled alongside my daughter Ilona and experienced the world through her acts of playing, and it continues now with my most inspiring colleague, Dr. Ilona Szekely, Professor of Art Education. The love and support from my wife Laura also helped make a rich and play-filled life possible.

CONTENTS

PREFACE

In this book I draw on two earlier publications, *Encouraging Creativity in Art Lessons* (1988) and *From Play to Art* (1991), to bring together key ideas in a new, up-to-date book for new times. The contents of the two books are merged and illustrated with a new set of images drawn from a wide range of 21st-century classrooms.

In this new volume I added a more complete discussion of the philosophical grounding of the value of play in art learning, including current research issues and references. The previous fine arts emphasis is extended by new sections on play and design and the potentials of play in teaching design innovation. I discuss the relevance of play and creativity in developing an interest and understanding of visual culture and examine how play and creative art teaching can be significant components in building critical thinking skills. I also added discussions about play, creative art teaching, and technology, including interdisciplinary art explorations, and explain in more depth how creative assessment practices in art could be integrated into traditional and current modes of assessment in a standards-based environment. Teacher support sections include discussions, field trips, Internet resources, and classroom activities in each chapter.

Overview of the Book

Chapter 1 introduces theories and research that support the understanding of play and its relationship to creativity and art. The reader is acquainted with the ideas of major figures in developmental theory, children's play, and creativity, as they relate to art education. Additionally, this chapter contains overviews of theories about play in art and the function of play in the classroom and ways to encourage play.

In Chapter 2 I look at play as a preparation for both teaching and learning art. This chapter focuses on the use of creative play as an appetizer for artistic inspiration and the search for ideas. The discussion of creative play themes at home is enlarged to reflect on play in school art classes and how creative play can become a foundation of school art. An introduction to play-based art teaching describes the role of students, parents, and teachers. In further analysis, play set-ups and performances are looked at as children's art, with significant connections to contemporary artists and their work.

Chapter 3 compares the child's studio at home and the typical art room. I explore the elements within those rooms that set the stage for curiosity and motivation to join in creative playing. The creation of fantasy and adventure settings focuses on visual surroundings that provide multisensory clues that call for physical and imaginative responses. In this chapter I recommend that art teachers give as much consideration to planning the art room space as they do to their lesson planning. A different kind of lesson planning is emphasized that draws on fantasy settings, playful material displays, and small but significant room changes to promote a variety of artistic and imaginative uses.

Chapter 4 looks at the materials that go into the creation of the play-centered art room. I combine overviews of the types of play materials art teachers can integrate into the art class with stories about how children find and use different materials in creative playing and art making. Children amass fortunes in interesting stuff that parents and teachers often consider valueless trash. I provide examples of play props ranging from the conventional to the unexpected as I explore the many resources children discover for found-object play.

In Chapter 5 I describe art rooms where active learners, action viewers, and fast-paced players create or experience art through movement. Children's art is motivated by all kinds of play, and even playful movements can be a source for their artistic expressions. Instead of designing spectator events for students based on passive consumption, the chapter suggests ways to initiate art room experiences where creative movement is an art and participation in movement play also inspires works in traditional art media.

Chapter 6 is about children's play themes that can inspire individual art classes and discusses how the play themes described should be an essential part of home and school art for all grades. They are "guaranteed" to withstand wear or change, and they are all subject to improvement by being stretched and altered by anyone willing to try them in original ways. All plays were tested, and indeed discovered, by children. Using thematic play as starting points allows teachers and students to transcend the traditional boundaries of art making and produce an entirely new range of art that questions what art is or could be.

Chapter 7 concludes the book with a discussion of how art teaching can be practiced as a way to foster innovation. Here I describe how art lessons can be challenging questions, innovative experiences, and independent investigations to view art in open ways. The chapter examines such themes as treating students as artists and players, searching for a contemporary art teaching model, or trying on the play artist's role.

For more information, ideas, and inspiration about play and creativity in art education visit

www.Playandart.org

www.creativeat.org

www.ArtTeaching.org

www.facebook.com/pages/Play-Based-Art-Teaching/1421378038108225

www.facebook.com/pages/Teaching-for-Artistic-Behavior-TAB/144118082280049

1
THEORY, RESEARCH, AND PURPOSE

FIGURE 1.0 Art teaching is a visual performance, a creative show and tell.

This chapter introduces theories and research that support the understanding of play and its relationship to creativity and art. The reader is acquainted with the ideas of major figures in developmental theory, children's play, and creativity, as they relate to art education. Additionally, this chapter contains overviews of theories about play in art and the function of play in the classroom and ways to encourage play.

Introduction

Twenty-five years ago, *From Play to Art* was published. The book resulted from my experiences playing with my three children and the creative inspirations that resulted, which changed my art and teaching forever. As an artist-educator I had long cherished free and playful inquiry in my painting, writing, and research. But it wasn't until I began actually playing with children that I understood the relationship between their play as art and art instruction. I wrote *From Play to Art* not from research in libraries but from notes taken at the playground and reporting from the floors of children's studios, their rooms. This book originally emerged out of many summers of playing in dirt piles, poolside, and inside an old children's playhouse on the hills of Woodstock, New York. Today, I still enjoy playing, now with my grandchildren, and I continue to discover new

FIGURE 1.1 Children's art is improvising with treasures on the floor.

connections between play and art. My passion to share new observations and lessons with future art teachers persists.

I can now report that children's play is not separate from art making. In fact, children's play is a form of art, a lively performance media, and in its many incarnations, play is the finest preparation for students of all ages to create unique and exciting works of art. Over 25 years of research in children's rooms, backyards, and schools, I learned how to revive playing in homes and school art classes in order to allow students to behave as artists.

One of the most important ways to achieve this revival is for parents and art teachers to embrace play with children. Leading and joining students in playing inspires artistic behavior for all involved; it makes for better parents, art teachers, and students. I urge parents and art teachers to become students of children's playing and creativity instead of basing school art on the principles and methods of teaching and making traditional or conventional adult art.

Just as the art world changes, so must art instruction and the way we look at children's art change. We must reform outdated ideas about traditional art making. Teaching art cannot only be based on lectures, readings, and research. It cannot only be based on observations of traditional school art classes. Fieldwork is important but needs to go beyond merely observing what has always been done in school art. Today's fieldwork for developing art instructors should include participatory observation of children during their most creative moments as they play in many ways that aren't limited to traditional art media.

As I noted in my very first book, *Encouraging Creativity in Art Lessons*, "Art teachers should not hesitate to depart from a world of citations and experts to freely observe children making art in all forms and media and freely reflect on the art teaching creative players require." This book summarizes what I continue to witness and find out through my spending time with the experts: young artists of all ages.

Starting a new book or a new series of artworks is a celebration of opportunities, of many blessings. The same can be said about starting every art class, which also has the potential to be a celebration of the gift of time and creative freedom. Being able to sit on the floor and engage the imagination is especially important during the fast pace of school days where every participant is busy and under stress. Each art class provides an opportunity for children to separate themselves from the structure of school life to do things differently, to create their art in a class that provides a safe haven for innovators.

Theories About Play

Understanding children's artistic development requires not just the study of stages in drawing but also looking at the unique ways artists grow as creative researchers and innovators using objects and the environment. The study of children's creative play presents a challenge to every art teacher and is an important part of the general field

FIGURE 1.2 Building fantastic playthings makes the art room the center of innovation in a school.

of developmental research. Greek philosophers Plato and Aristotle discussed the role of playing in education, but specific play theories were not developed until centuries later. The following briefly describes some modern theories and current trends.

Play as Therapy

In 1920, Sigmund Freud defined his psychoanalytic play theory in his book, *Beyond the Pleasure Principle*. Freud describes play as a child's mechanism for repeatedly working out a previously experienced traumatic event in an effort to correct or master the incident to his or her satisfaction. Play therapists today observe children's play to help diagnose developmental trauma and decide on remedial strategies.

Play and Social Development

Social development and play was linked in 1932 by Mildred Parten, who categorized play stages by describing children's social development. Parten uses the term "Onlooker Behavior" for young children who simply observe but don't join in playing. Infants and toddlers are called "Solitary Players," because they pay little attention to others while they engage in play, although they will occasionally interact through a toy. "Parallel Play" occurs when toddlers and two-year-olds use the same toys while sitting next to each other; they may talk to each other but about different topics. Their focus remains on individual play. What Parten described as "Associative Play" occurs during the early preschool years, as children collaborate more, share frequently, and engage in the play of others while still maintaining their own storylines and themes. In "Cooperative Play," older preschoolers share materials and make up stories together, assigning each other parts and roles in creating complex themes.

Play as Rehearsal

In 1972, Jerome Bruner specified that one of the main functions of children's play was to rehearse actions for different real life scenarios. Confronted in a safe and risk-free environment of play, difficult situations could be made to seem less stressful. Bruner's discussions illuminate play as a rehearsal for life.

Play as Life Preparation

Long before Bruner, John Dewey presented a similar view about play as a rehearsal for life, but in a more practical vein. Dewey was a prominent educational theorist in the early 1900s. According to Dewey, play is a subconscious activity that helps an individual develop both mentally and socially. Separate from work, play helps the child to grow into a working world. According to Dewey, as children become adults, they no longer need to play because they find amusement from their occupation. Play activities during childhood prepare everyone to become healthy working adults.

Play as the Child's Work

In the early part of the 20th century, Maria Montessori, a prominent Italian educational theorist, postulated that play is the child's work. According to the Montessori method, which continues to be employed today in many private schools, children are best served by spending their playtime learning. Montessori play is sensory, using a hands-on approach with everyday tools called "manipulatives" such as sandpaper letters. The student sets his or her own pace, and the teacher collaborates in helping the child play to learn.

Play and Cognitive Development

In the 1950s, psychologist Erik Erickson suggested eight stages of human development. Discussing the third stage, Erickson specifically speaks about play for preschoolers, which he calls "Initiative vs. Guilt." A child learns to imagine through active play and fantasy and to cooperate with others. In the fourth stage, "Industry vs. Inferiority," Erikson emphasizes the school-aged child's need to persevere and make things together. In this outlook, children progress from free play to teamwork, playing that is elaborately structured by rules.

Play and Intellectual Development

Jean Piaget is most noted for introducing stages of intellectual development. Perhaps his most notable work was defining cognitive development in play. Piaget's first stage is "Functional/Practice" play that involves repetitive muscle movements such as running, banging, or stacking. The second is "Constructive" play—for example, using blocks or materials to make things. The third, "Dramatic/Pretend" play, uses the imagination to role-play. In the final stage of "Games with Rules," children accept predetermined rules to play games such as chess or cards. According to Piaget, intellectual growth occurs as children go through stages of assimilation, manipulating the outside world to meet their needs through play-acting as they accommodate and adjust their views to meet the needs of the outside environment.

Dramatic Play

Play theorist Sara Smilansky wrote about dramatic play and its role in the child's development in 1968. Smilansky assessed dramatic play in terms of "Imitative Role Play," in which a child takes a make-believe role and uses imitative action and verbalization. "Make-Believe" is discussed with regard to objects, where toys that are not replicas of the object are substituted for real objects. "Verbal Make-Believe" refers to actions and situations. The child substitutes verbal descriptions for actions and situations. "Persistence in Role Play," occurs as the child continues within a role or play theme for at least 10 minutes. She also defines "Interaction" as dramatic play in which two players interact in the context of a play episode.

Play and ZPD

Lev Vygotsky (1970s) suggested that children use play as a means to grow socially. In play, they encounter others and learn to interact using language and role-play. Related to the topic of play, Vygotsky is most noted for introducing the ZPD, or "Zone of Proximal Development." He suggests that while children need to play with their playmates to grow, they need adult interaction to master each social skill and become ready to be introduced to new learning.

Art as Play, Play as Art

From the Parten study to the present, many stages in children's play, such as the development of language skills, physical and emotional skills, and cognitive and intellectual skills, have been investigated. George Szekely started the study of children's play by playing with his children and asking future art teachers to do the same. Szekely has been writing about play since 1975, examining creative play as a preparation for art. He views play as children's art, and he sees in this play-based art a foundation for invention and change that links childhood creativity to most innovations made by contemporary artists. Szekely believes that play focuses on the creative process, students' creative expressions of ideas, and open-ended experimentation in art. As creative players, students can prepare for art classes with materials and ideas and transform open-ended objects by self-prescribed investigation. Play is part of a life-long artistic behavior. For creative individuals in all fields, maintaining themselves as creative players is a life-long challenge and a goal for classes in art education.

What Is Play Art?

A winding line of children passes by the art teacher greeting them at the door. Everyone carries something, and the students are excited to come in and show and tell what is in their hands and on their mind. In a clearing at the center of the art room, students park their stuff, and the show begins. The first student shares a large woven basket she calls her "bathtub," which has a brown furry teddy bear occupant. As the story goes, her favorite playhouse is not the closet or under the bed but in the tub. With the help of the bear, she takes us on a small excursion pointing out the features to a typical playroom built in a tub. Everyone in the group follows the story with interest, and the art teacher is very supportive of the informal offer to construct this unusual playhouse.

FIGURE 1.3 From play to art: becoming a robot is amplified by drawings of the experience.

Defining Play Art

Children often refer casually to their play creations as "just making stuff." However, just because their creations are products of play doesn't mean they aren't art. Play art is the original, imaginative work of children. This multi-media art often predates drawings and paintings. Conceived and made in the process of imaginative play acts, children's art can be found in unrefined constructions, rich in original ideas. Play art reflects their individual interpretations of the world, like one child's vision of the future of cities shaped by candy bars collected after Halloween. While such models of real and fantasy worlds may look unsophisticated and hard to categorize in terms of traditional or conventional art, they are often some of the most original accomplishments in children's art repertory.

Encouraging Play Art

Play-based art is basically free from old master techniques, Bauhaus formulated art principles, or school art traditions. Play art is not the adult-directed art of polished bulletin board pieces. A child playing uses a free imagination to invent her or his own techniques and ways of constructing things. In playing, children are artists who freely use any object and theme to set up a vision. Thus, play-based art is unrestrained by art history, adult notions of art, or what has been done before. Art teachers should keep this in mind as they reflect on what children's art can be. What might art look like when it's created by children and not directed by adults? How is children's art different than the appearance of traditional art? Can we recognize the difference between art in school hallways and art made in home studios? As a model for guiding art in the classroom, future art teachers not only need to take a closer look at what children create on their own but also respect those creations as valid art.

Achieving Play Art

The finest examples of children's art are created through playing. Play art can be observed in the architecture of blocks and boxes, found-object furnishings for playhouses and playgrounds, or clever redesigns for everything that currently exists. Explored through unofficial design studies in playhouses or backyards, art appears in home chores such as setting tables and arranging groceries in the refrigerator. As I will discuss in more detail throughout this book, play art includes inventing games, making up new rules for everything, and demonstrating alternative ways everything can work. Play art is often evident in making toys, making real stuff, including gifts. It exists in impromptu scenes and props organized in actual spaces.

When one sees the nearly identical artworks that often line school hallways, one knows these works were created to fulfill an assignment, mimic a single technique carried out in the same materials. Such art projects a grasp of skill, not an exercise of imagination. Conversely, play art is created to fulfill students' fantasies and emerges from the exploration of a myriad of shared ideas. In this way, play creates many paths to original art, paths that cannot be traced to a single formulaic lesson. To make play art the class does not start with a mandate,

"This is what we're going to do today!" It begins with play, with an invitation to pretend: "Close your eyes and make believe . . . spread your wings and make a wish . . . draw in the air and let us guess your best idea." Creating art in a bathtub? What a great art studio and playhouse!

Play Is Art

"I am not good in art—I just like to play." Hearing the flagship artist of our family, my granddaughter Emilie, say that she is not good at art was strange. I hear this comment many times as an art teacher, but this was the first time I'd heard it from a highly experienced young artist who had been raised in the studio like she was. The occasion was a discussion over Emilie's preparation of a portfolio for admission into fourth grade of SCAPA, a public magnet school for art. With all the art teachers in our family, her confession was not easy to ignore. But, Emilie made her comment and continued to do what she had spent the whole morning working on: building an amazing candy store.

Unreservedly using the different recovered objects that jam our studio, Emilie set up laundry baskets as showcases for little jars filled with pencil shavings, candy pieces, and painted erasers. Between baskets, she made a counter out of yardsticks, a candy bag dispenser from tissue boxes, and filled an empty picture frame with her store sign. Being invited to the store's opening, I reminded Emilie that she said she was not good at art. "I just like to play and make things," she answered, as if her store installation was not art, just play. "Real art," she said, was required for admission to SCAPA.

So much of "real" art today is about play and discovery that students need to be aware that what they produce is not far from the "real" art world. Children need to be confident of their inventions, see them for the art they are. It is not inconceivable that Emilie's candy store and play-based pieces could be displayed in a modern art museum. Yet, the magnet school asks for shaded portraits and requires a 9×12 still life—very conventional and limited examples of art media.

An open view of art that includes play inventions needs to be a goal of art classes. In performing home chores, organizing play scenes and stages, arranging home performances, children create the future of art. In the play-based class students develop a respect for the arts that are seldom considered or thought of as art—namely, their own playing.

The Art World Is Changing

Calder's Circus (1921–1936), created by the artist Alexander Calder and currently showcased at the Whitney Museum represents a new type of sculpture. Unlike the fixed granite sculptures found in many museums, Calder's piece is mobile and dynamic. It features little wire circus entertainers and animals moving across the floor in scantily dressed scrap materials, performing in a freeform Circus ring. The figurines can be moved and rearranged according to whim.

Claes Oldenburg's exhibit, *The Store* (1961–64) is another groundbreaking example of sculpture that challenges assumptions about art. Now on display at New York's Museum of Modern Art, this collection of different grocery store product sculptures—from painted plaster hamburgers to pretend ice cream—reflects a spirit of play.

Work like Calder's and Oldenburg's bring us closer to understanding and appreciating the relationship between play and art as well as the groundbreaking works of children. Calder was a child-artist at heart, steeped in the exciting art of seeing children play with their toys on the floor. He created spontaneous characters from lunchtime leftovers and staged their play performances with simple objects he found on his studio table. Essentially, Calder's art helped usher in a new era that recognizes the value of play. This new era can be sustained by integrating the belief of play as art into art education practices.

The history of art education is a history of adult art. Even the most talented children's drawings and paintings are generally not considered art. Yet artistry is self-evident in the ways children play house, invent play foods, or put a detailed spoon figure to sleep in an eyeglass-case-bed. Today, we can view play as art with the hindsight of Earthworks, the land art movement; Happenings, varied types of performance art; Installations, or three-dimensional art exhibits; and even Flash Mobs. With new art styles like these, it seems that doors of today's art world are wide open to reconsidering what makes something art. It is understood that art does not have to be made with paints and brushes on fabric called canvas. Typically, these art styles have been named and popularized by adult artists; however, children made these breaks and utilized these new media in their play long ago.

If there were a comprehensive survey of the alternative art tools and practices children have invented, the history of modern art would have to be revised. For example, at great risk, children for generations have marked up walls in their home. Only recently have museums relocated their gold-framed treasures to make room for artists to express themselves directly on the wall. Only recently have the controversial creations of graffiti artists displayed throughout many large cities been lauded as "real" art. Great children's art in many forms of play have always existed but have been seldom praised as boundary-breaking art achievements. There is still little recognition in the art teaching community for the groundwork laid by children. Now that we see childhood play reflected in the work of so many artists, it's time to teach students to understand and take pride in their creativity, for other children like Emilie to recognize their play is their art.

Our Ideas About Play as Art Must Change

What was art before and what is art today provides few indications of what art will be tomorrow. The only certainty is change. Learning how to prepare students for the vast changes of art is the challenge that makes art teaching so fascinating.

When discussing and teaching art, we need to move beyond a focus on traditional or conventional art media to reflect on the many media and themes of players old and young. Students need to see the art that players create; this can include introducing them to the work of "professional" artists whose work references play, like Oldenburg and Calder, or this can include a great table setting made by a child for a teddy bear's tea party. Not only do the types of art students see need to be open but also the definitions of art need to be open. In play art, found objects, household items, and toys become art supplies. Canvases are all places in which children build play settings.

Children's play at home or outdoors has to be portrayed as art, meaning it must be respectfully talked about and presented to art students of all ages. Children can learn to see how art can happen at any time, when they complete chores or improvise performances with mundane objects. Children constantly originate new art forms in need of recognition. In the art of getting ready for school, all drawers and closets are opened like an artist's toolbox to design dozens of changes with patterns and colors. Beyond any stylist's dreams are hair styling plays that co-ordinate with hip-hop steps. On laundry days, children create free-form creases in ironing plays, then playfully make art by arranging a sock drawer and sculpting clothing piles. They apply artistic vision to all things in the home, keeping tabs on household trash to rescue anything discarded that can be turned into art. As we admire the technology-based artists of our day, it is important to observe how children approach phones and tablets most playfully as creative users.

At school, art also has to be unchained and opened to the art of playful inventions. Children can help us teach students to freely use everything and anything to wear or construct, to set up or perform with. Art teachers can expertly incorporate art rules, formulas, techniques, and lessons based on adult art and teach them through play. Play artists can make their mark on school art when they can bring all their play dreams, toys, and collections to class. Play as art has a golden age in early childhood and may never be seen again, unless wise art teachers become sponsors and brokers of playing, allowing it to flourish in art classes.

The Purpose of Playing in an Art Class

During my days as a substitute art teacher, I used to ask students what they were doing in art. They would respond like a chorus of trained seals, "We are doing Picasso!" Being new to the profession, I responded by instinct, "Only Picasso can do Picasso. My name is George, and I can only do George's art. Art is valuable because it's unique to each artist. No one else can do a Picasso or your art!" Early in my teaching, I learned that students think that doing art is like wearing a hand-me-down; it means grasping specific secrets passed down from the masters to our teachers and finally to us. I recall explaining to students that just like when they play, when they make art, they're doing something original. It comes from within, and it's theirs alone. To create original art, there needs to be room for children to play and assemble original experiences.

Play Provides Many Benefits

Play emancipates school art from a demonstration of "great art" and traditional adult techniques and examples, opening art up to young artists finding their own ways and means of doing things. Play is an alternative to the typical school experience, where everything is managed and predefined, made up of rules, how-tos, and approved actions. Players have fun trying everything and doing things differently without being held to art world conventions or school art standards from the past.

Play is the basis for maintaining the artistic confidence children generally have before entering school. This is because creative play allows for self-reliance and self-guidance, for shaping everything in one's own way. Also, because playing in art rooms alters attitudes towards school and school art. In playing, there are opportunities to search for and try out possibilities, to discover new media and art forms and set up models for ideas. Play in art rooms is necessary so that young artists can be in touch with their own art resources outside of school and thus reignite their confidence as artists.

Playing encourages self-discovery, an insight into self, surroundings, and relationships. To be a young artist takes not only the development of skills, but also a personal and emotional growth that play in art classes nourishes. Play releases the enormous tension and pent up emotions that easily build up in a highly regulated school environment. Playing affords some control over a difficult to control world and allows compensating with fantasy for what is sometimes a scary, hurtful, and difficult-to-predict reality.

Play makes art a personal statement and not just a school exercise. During play children divulge their secrets, and feelings about all the important people and things in their life. They express their likes and dislikes, fears, joys, even hostilities, providing a depth and purpose for art. The complex array of feelings and thoughts that occur in play are difficult to articulate, make sense of, or put into words; sometimes, they are more easily played out in artistic performances and images. Children play out a tangle of feelings with dolls, action figures, puppets, or trucks. Play makes school art into art, something that is personal, emotional, real, and important to its maker and powerful to view.

Play makes the art class authentic, more reflective of the individual creative process. Instead of starting with adult plans and instructions, play starts the art class with the way artists start: through self-discovery and the search for ideas. Playing starts the class with the young artist shopping, exploring spaces and settings, observing, and engaging their fantasies.

Play starts an art class with action, children's way of learning, discovering, and creating. It resists traditional school approaches by allowing students to move out of their seats, to inhabit floors, and explore under tables. Active hands and moving bodies promote touching and manipulating, sorting and organizing, building and destroying.

Play encourages positive socialization and interaction. While playing in an art class, children can exchange ideas or rehearse before others. They can also team up to get feedback on their ideas from their peers. By learning to provide feedback, children gain insights into their own inventions and ideas. Through play, the art room becomes a shared studio and a social space like a playground.

Playing in the art class models fun. It creates a mindset that having fun is acceptable, allowed in school, and a part of making art. In playing and having fun, students invent new roles, play with figures and objects, set up scenes and new locations, and enter fantasy worlds as part of their artistic journeys. Children play because it is enjoyable, but in their play, they discover ideas and a sense of purpose that further blossoms in many art forms.

Creative Play

It's 8 am, and students file into the art class unaware of what they will be doing. They look for clues on the board, waiting for the art teacher to announce the lesson. When everyone is seated, silence takes over, and the teacher announces the plan for the day. The students sit back and listen to what they will learn. Trained in art, the teacher holds the key to art knowledge and skills and decides on the daily agenda.

These students leave class holding identical projects to decorate the refrigerator door. They receive praise and good grades for following instructions and successfully doing what the art teacher had in mind. On the way out, they pass by the same project done by another class decorating the hallway bulletin board. The art teacher also receives praise for having such good ideas.

Next door in a play-based art class, students carry their discoveries: pockets filled with finds, bags of objects, and drawings. The students come to class excited to show and tell, to make and build things, and to invent and share their latest innovations. Excited to talk to the art teacher who greets them at the door, they cannot wait to reveal what they are thinking about and what they brought. They come prepared with stories because they trust that their teacher will be interested.

In the play-based art room, students cannot wait to share their many ideas. Their energy and playful suggestions start each art class. These students have learned that they have the best ideas, and the art room is the place where their ideas can be demonstrated. Here, students are the stars, and class begins with a discussion of architectural sketches of a Lego stadium constructed at home.

Leaving the play-based art class, students discuss their plans for home, what they will be doing next, and carry materials to work with. Art continues outside of the classroom with the "toys" they invented, which become objects to be enhanced, used, and played with after school. Their stuff is functional for play but also looks fun and unique, like the ice cream store one student carefully hugs. Another carries a belt-driven factory for constructing robots. In the hallway, one student talks about a car wash for Hot Wheels that will follow. The art class is just a pit stop for ideas on their way to even greater inventions after school. After leaving class, these students scout the hallways, picking up things they cannot wait to show and tell about during the next art class. A play-based art room inspires them to think about all the creative things to be done later.

Students come to a play-based art class to have fun. It's the only place left in school where that's still allowed. School imposes not only posted rules but also unstated guidelines for moving, behaving, and thinking. Playing in an art room allows students to move, act playfully, and think openly. Playing recaptures joys and provides opportunities for children to be children. They can do amazing things, like move around and find things in a room that are entirely theirs to use. Some students call art class their indoor playground; others say it's the school's center for invention and creativity.

Play-based art classes welcome raw materials and both provide space and offer support for student designers and innovators in all grades. In playing, students take the lead and provide the details for what is to be done. Students are collectors, shoppers, planners, and experts, having logged many play hours in home studios, in kitchens, backyards, or at the beach. In a play-based art room, students build not just models but gain confidence as individuals with valid ideas, a belief in themselves as creative people, inventors, and artists.

As the last bastion in school for fun and exploration, the art class provides a special room that runs on students' ideas, where toy worlds can be built. Students need the space, opportunity, humor, and patience a play-based class provides to develop their creative capacities and imagine their unique worlds, so they can experience what their lives can be like with art as part of it. Parents of students in play-based art classes say, "My daughter now is always the first to suggest creative solutions to anything." "He has become a proud idea person," a mother affirms. "My son wants to be an inventor and likes that his art teacher calls him that in school."

Playing in the Art Class

Creative play opens the way to freedom in art. By liberally practicing play, students realize that anything is possible. In a play-based art class, everything can be played with: anything can be touched and tried, explored and built with, taken apart and investigated, worn, animated, set up, or knocked down. Anything can be drawn on or painted with, enlisted as a canvas, tool, or media. Players can work outside the proverbial lines. They can move anywhere in a room or on a canvas and try what has not been done before. Playing demonstrates that creativity has few bounds; everything can be rebuilt, redesigned, and reinvented. Nothing is off-limits to players: everything is possible and nothing is too crazy or out of the question.

Creative play moves the understanding of art from skill or talent—being able to draw SpongeBob correctly—to thought, where art means ideas, being inventive, and making anything one can imagine. Play is forward-looking; it's the future of art. It allows young artists to see things in novel, uninhibited, and unique ways. Play is a bridge to contemporary art and the ability to enter future art worlds. Play allows students to see themselves as creating the new in art and being the artists of the future.

Creative play also provides opportunities for visual brainstorming. Students can mine from discarded piles, pass their finds around, and compare ideas for their uses. In this way, playing challenges creative thoughts. Showing what could be done with an object, making it work, talk, and walk before an audience generates possibilities. Playing means auditioning objects, showing how objects everywhere can play many parts. Players of the world unite in the theater of art class to manipulate, set up, and explore everything as a potential part of art.

Promoting Creative Play

As a space of the potential, the play-based art class has nothing to do with art supplies and everything to do with the ability to play with every object and determine what makes it interesting. This makes students experts of the imagination, in securing junk, building with anything, and turning trash into playable treasures. Players bring their finds to class and keep each other informed of places where unusual things can be found. The classroom thus functions as a marketplace to exchange the overlooked or underappreciated, for items that would never be seen or brought to explore in school. Creative players pick from the floor or freebies from the market, evoking a thousand ideas for what to do! Students fill bags and sketchbooks with things that could never function as traditional school and art supplies. The art room needs to be the place to do it, where there is support from an adult willing to listen and help make it happen.

When students are permitted to collect and choose, they show a surprising taste in unusual, playable forms. Creative players design with bread crust and build bagel towers. Their building materials are as unique as the forms they create. Unconcerned with the intended use of any object they play with, they make everything their own. Lampshades are worn as fashion items and cherries used as paint.

Play with interesting objects of all kinds stimulates creative thinking for all ages. Forms and toys that are open and least structured contribute the most opportunities to innovate. Young children don't need instructions to find interesting ways to use anything. For school age children not used to playing, props that leave too much to the imagination can induce anxiety because they won't know what to do, and they tend to focus on playing "the right way." This makes practicing artistic shopping throughout a student's school years essential, as when they freely gather found objects and then brainstorm about their use, or when they find their own supplies for each project and art class.

Ultimately, promoting creative play means student instincts need to be trusted and their suggestions listened to. Students need to be placed in charge of finds and discoveries and suggestions for what to do. After all, creative play is children's own media. It provides young artists a comfortable way to think about, talk about, and make art. Play does not cloud art ideas with principles, rules, traditions, and ways one art is to look or supposed to be made. Play provides the opportunity to practice creative independence, for self-initiated projects to flourish. This is why students as players are children with many good ideas. These young artists are not technicians or specialists in one computer program, art tool, or process, but they feel they can do and make anything: a good preparation for contemporary art.

A General Outline of the Play-Based Class

Looking at *Art News* magazine on the kitchen table, my granddaughter Emilie thoughtfully examines the sculpture on the cover. With a marker in her hand, she comments about the abstract sculpture: "I think it would look better with some belly button rings." She proceeds to sketch over the abstract sculpture, even adding wheels and a string to the square base.

The freedom to re-envision the world, including contemporary art, comes from a child who is ready to play with everything. Below, I have sketched a brief outline of what a play-based art class involves, providing basic recommendations that I will expand throughout this book.

In a Play-Based Art Class

The teacher is not solely responsible for preparation and planning. Students must also come prepared with collections, plans, and ideas, and preparation occurs outside of class.

Any object can be an art supply and freely integrated into play, no matter what the object's original purpose.

Students use things such as found objects, furnishings, space, light, and sound to create their art.

The word "art" does not hamper explorers in art classes. Student art consists of making toys, building objects, pretending, embarking on play-adventures, and much more.

Students are empowered to be independent thinkers and performers, to be self-reliant and self-directed, and to make things of their choosing.

Students take risks, experiment. They are free to be messy and illogical; to believe in the magical; to explore through building and performing.

Students play in the room or use the community and environment as their canvas.

Students are encouraged to be open-minded and able to visually brainstorm, uncovering the potential of art.

Teachers and students use play to question the sacred and reexamine the basics of art and art education.

Ultimately, the play-based art class encourages the freedom to re-envision and innovate necessary to prepare a child to play with anything and everything in the world, including contemporary art.

Addressing Obstacles to Play and Art

Not all children receive the support they need to embrace and practice play to develop their creativity and independence. In fact, much of our culture inhibits their artistic development through excess structure and regulation of children's lives. Structure becomes overly emphasized for four reasons. First, play isn't recognized as a valid entrée into art. Second, children's creations aren't recognized as art. Both of these reasons are based on the assumption that creating art is a serious, adult activity, and I address this in the section on "Play Is Art." Third, play isn't encouraged because allowing for the freedom to play requires demands efforts that adults can't always make. Finally, not everyone understands the benefits of play or how to encourage it. I address these latter assumptions here.

Attitude

Adult attitude towards play sends signals that children pick up on. Some adults are insecure about their own creativity, which can affect the emphasis they place on children's playing in general. This may be because those adults never had an immersion in playing, and they lack the experience to be free with their imagination or embrace the messy world of play. Others may have lost contact with their playful self and cannot reach out to pretend and explore with children. Or maybe they worry about losing their position as authority figures.

Some adults view play with admiration, but that view can quickly turn to exasperation. Floor-crawling investigators, for example, are applauded, but when they invade kitchen cupboards, they are barely tolerated before the doors are locked. Children's rooms and play areas are first allowed to be used freely, but only until it becomes time to clean up, to organize. In these instances, play is embraced when it fits a schedule, designated to appropriate times and areas, but then it is discouraged during other times.

Some adults think that play is only for young children and that after a certain age, play equals immaturity. Suddenly, toys and other creativity-inspiring objects are discarded, and playrooms become home offices or TV rooms.

Some adults try to be encouraging of their children's artistic development but promote more traditional art media, like paintings and drawings, something they can display on the fridge. Art that the child can't display, like role-playing, pretending, is harder for parents to sit down and take the time to celebrate.

Space

As much as adult attitude, the physical environment such as the size of the play space, what is allowed in it, or who is in charge of it affects the chance for, and development of, play. Some children have their own room, the privacy of their own studio to set up displays and store collections, a space they are allowed to control. Most children, however, do not. Particularly children in low-income families, where there may be few things in the home that can be played with or there may be little space to play.

Rigid Ideas

Play is generally much more tolerated at home and then systematically erased at school. Art becomes separate from play, and art is presented through techniques and principles, not experimentation and exploration. Play creations and expressions of creative ideas in most media are dismissed or disassociated with art. Toys, the experimental touch, playful behaviors, and performance are not considered "serious" art and are banned as childish, a distraction from real learning. Traditional adult art in well-established, conventional art media becomes the preferred and celebrated goal.

Approaches to art in school tend to be rigid and hierarchical rather than flexible and cooperative. Art teachers bring their own project ideas and lesson plans to class for students to execute. Only certain art materials and tools are considered appropriate, and they can only come from vendors or the art teacher. The gap between play and art widens as play, which was the essence of the preschool child's art, looks and feels very different than the art talked about in school. As children don't show or talk about their home art in class, they start to disregard those creations as valid art, and their belief in themselves as generally creative people diminishes. Teachers often unwittingly encourage this diminishing confidence when they don't see their students as already artists, when they don't rely on or trust student abilities. The art teacher is the artist in an art class, not the students.

Art classes rely on an academic and formulaic approach. Art lessons have become the modern Legos that purport to be creative, but provide instructions for proper use. The formulaic art teachers present to students leaves little room for what students like, what they feel, think about, or collect. It attempts to turn them into art robots. So students are left with only vivid play memories to cherish, hiding them along with the play objects they are not supposed to bring to class.

Removing Obstacles

Adults generally mean well, but they can inadvertently stifle a child's imagination and impetus toward creativity and art production. But there are ways that adults can reduce the obstacles that discourage play and foster play's beneficial influence on developing artists.

First, adults might want to recognize that in play, they do not have to be in charge. In fact, it might be useful to think of the child as the leader and the adult as the follower, where the adult takes direction and cues in order to become more familiar and comfortable with play.

Adults can also learn to embrace the creative chaos. I will address this issue in more detail next chapter. Those who value play welcome active and noisy kids who want to touch and play test everything. When adults recognize play as art and children as artists, they can create every opportunity for hands-on exploration, inventing with blocks and found objects. They will set up rooms for independent exploration, play-acting, and active performing.

Even if there is no room for the children to have privacy, homes and classrooms can be made to feel more open by letting the child freely access everything in the space, so they are comfortable using and borrowing anything. The main thing to remember at this point is that a child's habits are formed early, and limitations beyond safety considerations can severely inhibit the development of play.

Ultimately, adults must respect children's processes and authority and avoid criticizing as much as excessive directing. Only young artists really know, or fully understand, the connections between their play and art, and they may or may not want to tell you. A young artist's mind and work to some degree are mysteries to be respected and not analyzed or directed by the art teacher, who is basically an audience. Art teachers should be extremely cautious about making judgments about the thoughts and imaginative works or ideas of others. We need to be very modest and careful about our assessment of art students, such as knowing who is creative, or who will be an artist, not judging artistic skills or its development. How much can we ever know what is in the minds, in the plans, in the dreams of a child playing, a young artist in class? Yet, many adults criticize as if they can fully comprehend, accurately know, and even measure what goes on in an individual's playful state and creative act.

Cultivating Artists, Not Robots

Adults would also do well to recognize that children need to keep playing at all ages to avoid becoming art robots. Play at home and in the art room, whether for preschoolers or teens, allows their art to remain authentic and unique. Playing with found objects and simple toys that come without instructions at home and in school develops the imagination necessary for children to be creative people, builders and innovators. Playing in art means being faithful to children's imagination, means letting them rely on their own creative ideas instead of relying on Disney or the latest video games or school-appointed projects.

In art, play serves as a transformation of reality in the service of the creative self. When play is regularly encouraged at home and in the classroom, creative transformation becomes a life-long habit. This is because artists tend to be independent learners, self-guided. Play can be an important tool in seeking self-generated creative ideas for any task. A player will not wait for a lesson, they are anxious to develop and showcase their own inventions, collections, and ideas. That is why we must do all we can to preserve the benefits of play for children of all ages.

The Stages of Creative Play

In this section, I address stages of development to help teachers and parents plan various approaches to integrating play. After all, even discussions about being original and playful should be easily sequenced according to what is age-appropriate. Unlike traditional discussions about best practices that tend to be based on quantifiable data and statistics, discussions about art and play—activities that require the freedom to let go, to move, paint, or write unencumbered—must be based on alternative information and sources, as quantifying creativity is difficult.

While working on this book, my sources of information came from my granddaughters and my advisors for the project with whom I discussed play and creativity. Other sources come from my lectures about play and discussions with colleagues. I paint my suggestions regarding the development of creative play for different age groups with broad strokes and the requisite understanding that what is creative and playful—like writing a book—does not necessarily take form in logical steps or stages, and creativity and play continue throughout our lifetime.

Early Childhood Play

Between the ages of one and three, play is a practice of individual communication and learning. Children are full time players and explorers beholden mainly to their own interests and desires. Around this time, children start to play with other children and become more aware of what their associates do. A child might not join their peers, but they get more curious about what they are doing and making. Children may begin to cooperate by handing over a toy or found object that someone else's artistry requires.

By the time they reach approximately four or five, children are more likely to act as full associates and partner with others to take on the larger challenges of self-assigned play. By this age, most children are ready to cooperate and become members of artistic teams. However, for many, individual playing remains the ultimate pleasure and will remain important for the life of a solitary artist.

Children from one through five physically change from exploring floors by crawling to becoming stand-up performers. They progress from low dexterity—using primarily large muscles—to greater dexterity and the ability to use smaller objects and tools for detailed activities. They don't necessarily abandon their large brushes or stop painting with a mop or "drawing" with a rake, but they gain access to a greater range of tools with which to create.

Over the journey of the first five years, sensory exploration declines as language takes dominance and leads to social play. Social play often starts with family-play as the child recruits partners of all ages "to play mommy and daddy." As children process interest in and awareness of larger worlds, their play expands to the social networks of their whole neighborhood. They start to play bank, post office, or restaurant, modeling and pretending to be in all places used to shop or dine.

During this period, the scope and dimensions of play space change from crib, high chair, or the confines of a shopping cart. With mobility, being able to crawl and walk, children adventure over increasingly larger areas of the home and outdoors, giving them more space in which to imagine and play. On excursions with parents, there are more things to find and pocket, so they gain access to more objects to test and explore. Every routine or special family trip becomes an opportunity for treasure hunting and exploring spaces to play-test everything.

Preschool Play

As the size of playgroups increase with age, play becomes richer in invention with complex use of voices, figures, and props.

In playing school and instructing a Barbie art class, there are many participants and elaborate settings created. At this time, observing developmental changes is important; children using the same play materials do so differently at different ages. Early play fosters vital roots to be built on later in school. Play using cars or blocks or involving dressing up later becomes play designing cars, cities, and fashion runways. Upper elementary classes play circus and demonstrate a variety of acts such as a troupe of talented elephants that paint. Middle school students might cooperate to design Dinosaur World, an interactive film and exhibit. Knowing that younger children typically play in isolation, while older children integrate play into cooperative social activities, is useful for creating appropriate play opportunities.

Pretend play occurs more in the later preschool years, and its functions are many. They include simple imitation of adults, intensification of real life roles, reflection on home relationships, expressions of pressing needs, forbidden impulses, and the reversal of roles such as playing teacher. Dramatic play has many affective, intellectual, and social benefits for the preschool child. The central roles in young children's dramatic play are family parts. Children assume a variety of characters and functional roles: "you will be the dog," "I am a super hero," "I am a dancer and you are the audience." Creativity and invention contain the important component of active performance and pretending that suffer when play and active improvisation are left out of education.

Children's habits of play before they enter school are influenced by many factors, including a child's history of playing with their parents or other adults. While children play, some adults read the paper and otherwise act as adults. Some adults engage in only a few activities with the child. They may play wrestle or sports, yet they prefer not to play-act/pretend, build things, or use their imagination.

Luckily there are adults who enthusiastically embrace the opportunity to play again and tell stories of their childhood. These individuals generally feel comfortable getting down on the floor and connecting with the child's playing. Youngsters welcome adults they perceive as willing to watch and participate, someone they can always ask to join in playing. They respect supportive and helpful adult playmates who don't direct or take over events.

Primary School/Elementary Play

Full-time schooling presents new opportunities and challenges for integrating and facilitating play. Most children are ready for school by age six or seven. At this age, they tend to be more prepared as creative players than students. Ideally, over many years of preschool playing, children accumulate important creative experiences and develop their creative intelligence. They figured out how to organize their thoughts by making their ideas come to life, either through pretend or through building, and they explored the future by problem solving and modeling. By the time they come to school, many children have been members of design teams and invented group games. Before elementary school they engaged in creative private and public performances and used play that balanced emotion with intellect. Early artistic play dealt with feelings, captured observations, explored ideas, and built on memories.

The school environment, on the other hand, tends to value intellect over emotion and requires more structured and logical problem solving. Students are expected to learn order and to follow instructions in the classroom, and the time for students to maintain their skills as competent artistic players generally becomes reserved for after school. Aside from this school for work/home for play divide, two changes that occur when students start school have a larger impact on a child's creative development.

First there is a social change that occurs for children during the elementary years. Peers become more important and children's play reflects this great need to belong. The ages of their friends make a difference in how they play, depending on whether those friends are younger, the same age, or older than they are. Friends influence play choices that may vary from video games to active floor play that involves pretending and constructing. The games played with school friends affect children's play interests and, thereby, the fate of creative play.

Second, there is often a change in after-school activities that affects children's social circles and how they will play. Play art is enhanced for children who come home after school and have plenty of free time to excavate the backyard or build forts and clubhouses with friends. With no prescribed extracurricular engagements, they can rely on their imagination to guide them. Other children are heavily loaded down by after-school activities and friendships that revolve around physical activities like soccer or dance lessons. They have little creative playtime and few opportunities to make up their own games and rules. How children spend after-school time shapes their ability to flourish as inventive players at home and in school.

Ensuring time for play in the art classroom ensures the continued engagement of a child's imagination and creative energies at a time when so many other changes can interfere with or interrupt the development of their ingenuity and creative resourcefulness. The art classroom can provide the balance they need between academic structure and artistic freedom. Ultimately, elementary students should be encouraged to foster both orderly thinking and their tolerance for disorder, the random and accidental. They can learn about logic, but they need to continue to take leaps into the illogical, be able to bring together unrelated forms, and transform objects to suit imagined play visions. Elementary students are not just scholars, but also artists, players, and inventors of the new.

Play in the art class not only helps students balance their skills but it also helps them develop self-esteem, which becomes very important in the formative school years. Children need to demonstrate to themselves and others that they have skills, abilities, and talents they can be proud of. Influenced by the academic lessons they experience as students, play at this point in their development tends to become more industrious. Children seek to accomplish something and to have a product to share. Effective art instruction can ensure students become as proud of their art play as they are of academic or sports accomplishments. Art teachers can build players' self-esteem by focusing on childrens' achievements and praising their creative ideas, playful manipulations, collections, interests, and inventions. In contrast to achievements based on conformity in the academic classroom, art teachers can help students see the benefit of achievements through artistic behaviors based on the ability to maintain oneself as a creative player and independent thinker, a person with unique plans and ideas, someone who can make and build inventive projects helps to build a proud artistic personality.

While most schooling underutilizes or discourages artistic play, art class can provide students with opportunities to perform as children, using play for learning and discovery. As play practice is shut down in favor of learning lead by adults, the art class can provide a balance and awaken independent thinkers with access to original ideas. The intellectual development demonstrated by this age group can stretch to using play as the artistic intellect. The most important part of an art class is to foster and preserve all the creative and inventive abilities children come to school with that become undernourished by general education.

Secondary School Play

In their intellectual development, the adolescent moves from concrete forms of reasoning to the abstract and hypothetical. As children get older, they make greater efforts to adapt to reality rather than distort reality in art or play. In social terms, teenagers move toward independence, and in the move away from parents seek the protection and safety of peer groups. They also single out particular individuals to "hang" with and have close relationships.

Struggling to create a stable and permanent sense of self, play offers teens a low-stakes form and context for the kind of experimentation that can help them establish a strong identity. A peer group of artists, players, and explorers can aid a teen's search for independence and uniqueness, can respond to a teen's inner needs in the way that the structured classroom can't. This is why unstructured opportunities for play remain important to a teen's development. Unfortunately, because they are struggling to develop their identity, teens suffer from a reputation of being unmanageable and unruly. They are also assumed to be naturally conformist, afraid of standing out, wanting to just melt into the crowd. Because of this, school classes, including art, become more regulated in an effort to control these young students.

So, on one hand, the teen is better able to fantasize, invent, and work abstractly. They seek to establish their individuality, self-reliance, and to be recognized. They want to exercise their skills and search for meaningful things to do. On the other hand, middle and high school classes establish stricter rules and assign more concrete projects. They also clamp down on and herd students in school 'teams.' Thus, secondary schools do not convey a sense of trust in students and give them fewer opportunities to just do their thing.

However, many adolescents yearn to be themselves, make personal choices, and express their uniqueness. They want to be trusted and given free reign. Teens find all of this and more in the art of creative playing. In a play-based art class, students assert their independence, act as artists, and take control of planning the direction of their efforts and art. Students test their wings as designers and inventors, architects, filmmakers, and futurists. They are free to be silly or unexpected. Like the teens I witnessed, they can play on the floor, design "funky" hats with which to pretend, bring old appliances to take apart and rebuild into robotic fantasies. This is because the play-based art class gives teens a pass to explore, to briefly release themselves from aspirations toward adulthood because art—unlike other schoolwork—doesn't 'count.' When really, this freedom is what counts the most.

Beyond School Play

Play starts in childhood but needs to be fostered throughout a person's life. A lifetime of fun and invention can begin during early childhood and move into art classes that engage creative players. The best way to ensure that play remains part of a child's life—thereby ensuring creative interests as an adult—is to integrate it in private home life and public school life.

To understand how play can enter into daily life, let's look at breakfast. Even setting the table can become an opportunity for invention. Two sisters, ages four and six, set a breakfast table, using different color dishes and experimenting with utensil arrangement. In spite of their age difference, they are both able to play with every chore as an art opportunity. Playing at breakfast, they act as artists as they learn to invent with tiny dishes in different playhouses. For this kind of play to work, it must be encouraged, celebrated, meaning that sometimes order and tradition must be overlooked. After all, in a home and art class where funny settings are celebrated (and not corrected), more original play acts will follow. Here are three more examples that demonstrate different generations of players starting a day, making art out of routine.

A preschool child opens a package of bagels. Before thinking about cream cheese she decides to build a bagel tower. The new architecture is admired and knocked down to make room for a fresh canvas. This time bagels are balanced over a cup. The top hole is decorated with a flaming red napkin. For the preschool child everything is a toy, a playful building block, and an art supply. Her expressions in bagels are an example of how play art develops.

The elementary age child eats a poppy seed bagel over a white paper plate. The plate highlights the spreading of millions of unique speckles. "It's the universe in space!" She rotates the plate for a moving experience, presenting her creative piece to everyone at the table. The older child discovers art in an everyday event that can be titled, translated, and demonstrated in action. Play is a display of her creative powers, generating ideas in seeing possibilities in everything.

Dad plays with food. He turns his bagels into eyeglasses. Caught up in an investigative play, Dad mounts bagel wheels on the sleek napkin dispenser to drive it around the plate. This bagel talk fosters three generations speaking to each other in one of the many languages of play. An intergenerational model for viewing home as art class filled with a family of players. Transforming and finding new ways to play with ordinary objects, actively playing with everyone and with everything in hand, life becomes an art class that continually centers around creativity.

All-Ages Play

Ultimately, play leads to fresh insight for all ages and all stages of creative life. In fact, to engage in art and play activities gets to be more important as one becomes older and further removed from just doing it intuitively. As one moves from the highchair and becomes less inclined to be messy, to believe in magic, to engage in silly dreams and crazy behaviors, play becomes essential to one's ability to arrive at something new and significant.

2

BEGINNING THE ART LESSON

Inspiration and Preparation

FIGURE 2.0 Art can be a child's prized play object.

In a fast-changing art world, contemporary art education should have deep roots founded on children's imaginative and spontaneous play. It is true that most children stop playing at different points in time as they enter school, but play needs to continue. Throughout the school years, the study of young children's wide ranges of creative play can guide parents and teachers from kindergarten to twelfth grade. Instead of modeling art education on the works of adults and art principles, children should be recognized as unique artists and their art and play used as a guide to school art.

This chapter looks at play as a preparation for both teaching and learning art. It focuses on the use of creative play as an appetizer for artistic inspiration and the search for ideas. The discussion of creative play themes at home is enlarged to reflect on play in school art classes and how creative play can become a foundation of school art. An introduction to play-based art teaching describes the role of students, parents, and teachers. In further analysis, play set-ups and performances are looked at as children's art, with significant connections to contemporary artists and their work.

Traditional Art Skills Versus Play Skills

Children have a distinct approach to play and art that is different from adults. They are likely to do their best independent playing and art-making before they enter school. The goal of school art should be to foster this independent creativity and maintain playful actions and thinking that empower invention and the imagination.

FIGURE 2.1 Art is making the things one needs, such as a bed for a favorite doll.

Fostering Traditional Art and Limitations

Adults send children to school to teach them how to think and behave like grown-ups, and this includes the art classroom where children are taught to make art like adults. Rather than learning to explore, to see and think creatively, children learn to use conventional art processes and follow traditional rules and principles to essentially make adult art. Because of this, art becomes like other school subjects where they learn to do as they are told in order to get a good grade. In the process of learning the game of school, children forget that they have great ideas and forfeit playful behaviors and artistic thinking.

Some children can succeed in school art and become skillful at producing the kind of traditional art that gets presented to them. Unfortunately, other students struggle because they are unable to master traditional skills. They experience humiliation, frustration, fear, and become discouraged, feeling that they are not good in art and art is not for them. They opt out of future art classes by claiming they are not talented or find other ways to get out of the "art business" for the rest of their lives.

During the school years, many students learn little that is useful to sustain them as creative individuals who can be confident in their ideas. The way art is taught like any other subject destroys children's curiosity and their unlimited courage to make and discover art on their own. School art has its short-term rewards for some, but in the long run the rules taught are limiting, taking a long time to unlearn. Being forced into traditional art learning molds, children grow to have a narrow and limited view of art, and move away from the free and playful inventors they should have become. Art teachers who learn from what they observe in art classes that focus on traditional art skills only end up replicating the stifling cycle in their own classrooms.

Fostering Play and Possibilities

The alternative is to learn from children's creativity in their home playing and art experimenting. This way, art teachers and parents can understand the conditions and spirit in which children do their best art, and they can tailor art experiences to fit the way children already naturally create, explore, and experiment.

In an art class, children need to grow not only in their knowledge of art, but in curiosity, confidence, independence, and the courage that it takes to continue to be a child, a player, and an artist for the rest of their lives. Throughout this book, I offer descriptions of children at play being great inventors and creators. Instead of explaining, or forming theories, I cite examples of observations. This is what art teachers need to do for themselves: get to know children by playing with them, learning from their plays, and appreciating their great inventive powers.

It is vital for play-based art teachers to rethink art education from the perspective of their own childhood and from watching other children. This necessarily implies doing more than field observations in school art classes and making sure that future art teachers informally interact with children; only then can teachers learn to find ways to bring play situations, fun, and examples of creative exploration to the art room. Playing with children on the floor is important in learning to trust students, to support them in art classes without trying to change them, or just offer information about art and artists.

It is interesting to know what goes on in the left and right side of the brain, how experiences are stored, but it is not the essence of learning to become an art teacher. What art teachers need to know is what has been known for a long time: play, creativity, and art are mutually supportive activities and work best when unforced. Vivid, vital, and pleasurable play experiences are the easiest way to make an art class unforgettable and something children want to return to.

Play Skills for a New Art Curriculum

We create poorly and form bad opinions about our creative ability when we think about art unfavorably and perceive the nature of art badly, when we are anxious and afraid of it in school. Playing in art classes can allow a fearless ingenuity and bold invention. When children are afraid, art learning stops dead in its tracks. When an art class is fun, everyone learns freely.

Play and art have a distinctive contribution to the school curriculum. What is to be appreciated and preserved in art classes is the uniqueness of young artists at play. Art needs to come from students, rooted in their particular expressions of ideas and innovations. An art class is a place to learn about the future of art and design that can be seen from the best vantage point, observed in the play of children.

Play as Preparation for Art

Before school, my granddaughter Emilie and I warm up our creative spirits. From across the kitchen, she sees me dial on a banana and make ringing sounds. Knowing there's always a moment to spare for play, Emilie reaches to select her own phone from the fruit bowl, and a humorous conversation ensues.

Playing sets the mood, making everything that follows just as silly, light-hearted. While on the phone, Emilie is invited to help empty the buzzing dishwasher. Wearing a mixing bowl over her head, because now she's an alien, she opens

FIGURE 2.2 Building a dream bed is an admission ticket to a wealth of fantasies.

the kitchen cabinet. Blowing the horn for clearance, I drive from the dishwasher using a pot cover as steering wheel. We race each other around the table, blowing our horns. Now, Emilie's play spirits are fired up, and I am in the proper mood to get on the floor with my classes.

Play as Preparation for Teaching

The study of children's play and art requires close participation, observation, and creative ideas, so it can be applied to school art. Child study, experiences in home play and home art, need to be as important as student teaching, which is the study of school art. Required hours spent in children's home studios and community play settings can be a highlight and long-term inspiration in the education of art teachers.

Creating playful states for everyone is the art teacher's challenge. People often assume that growing up requires curbing one's enthusiasm and curiosity in all forms. However, the art classroom is where people can learn to hold onto their playful inclinations and inquisitiveness. Adults and students alike benefit from being allowed to be silly and playful, but how do art instructors encourage students who are forced to be serious and devoid of action or emotion in school to be playful in a classroom if the instructor can't be playful? First, those art instructors need to be taught to embrace their own imaginatively free ways. This change can be brought about by animating teacher education classes, getting would-be teachers out of their seats or down onto the floor, so they can rehearse future playful roles.

Teaching Play as Preparation for Art

Class begins with everyone making funny faces at each other, testing different distorted expressions on each other. Funny faces evolve into portrait making that begins with putting on make-up and Post-it Note features. Bodies then contort and mold in a free-form Twister to suggest stories and portray images. Some bodies take off for a flight around the room, and flapping arms wind up funny moods. Such play acts evoke silly, creative thoughts and actions in any form. While such behaviors are generally frowned upon in school, the art classroom accepts playing with banana or a mixing bowl, or making faces, making it a welcoming place for innovative shakers and movers.

To turn a classroom mode up to a high state of play readiness requires doing the unusual, engaging in the unexpected. School teaches control and discipline: keeping bodies silent, hands still, and thoughts rational. School regulations impose seriousness in thoughts and purposeful moves for prescribed learning. However, the creative behaviors required for playful art making cannot occur on demand. Silly improvisations can set the scene and invite funny thoughts and a range of playful responses. For example, you can imagine a pretend carrier pigeon to send invitations or knock on the door and deliver a singing telegram by teddy bear. Creativity happens when the soil is prepared by play and the environment suggests the imagination can take root and grow. The illogical and irrational, the unexpected and out of place in school are preparations for innovation.

An art teacher should never be afraid of getting a laugh by saying something funny, striking a rare pose, or putting on something silly. Saying the unexpected and doing silly things keeps play and creativity in art classes flowing. Playful art teachers dare to move beyond art principles, teaching techniques, and adult solemnity to do lots of pretending and imaginary play-acting. Wear a clown nose and try on brightly patterned fabrics. The students, also wearing bright red noses, can contribute by helping you formulate a clown suit from the scraps. Students can then start their own dress-up competition to audition for the circus. Teaching through live-modeling play nourishes fun. Creating an art class where everything is possible requires a public willingness to take risks and attempt the unimaginable. This willingness to tickle the imagination with the unconventional demonstrates the foundation of this class to be so different from other school classes.

Lessons From Children

Since playing with children is the most direct way of learning to appreciate their unique art, I've decided to share some of my own experiences. The following segments offer a supplement to the previous section on observing play, and they are descriptions of some of the lessons I've learned after a winter holiday break spent playing with my 6-year-old granddaughter Danielle.

FIGURE 2.3 Play art can be worn and carried along, joining different media and performances.

Preliminary Shopping

On the way to our house from the airport, I offer Danielle a free pass to shop at our local arts and crafts store. The pass is redeemable for items of her choice. What she puts in her cart is vastly different than what I would buy for an art class. She calls it "play stuff to make things with." We check out sparkly letter stickers, shimmering foam sheets, carefully selected ribbons, shiny buttons, and paint markers. It's important for artists to make their own selections and art teachers to be aware of children's choices.

A Studio Within the Studio

In my studio, Danielle picks out her spot. She asks for containers to be her designated supply boxes. With great ceremony, she unwraps all her gifts and thoughtfully begins a long process of admiration and sorting. After deciding on materials, she selects a place to play and decides what to do first. Danielle wants to set up in the closet. She organizes her own space, creating a studio within the room. Danielle's work is the same as any artist's: she chooses what to play with, where to play, and what to do. These are also primary considerations in preparing for an art class.

Early Morning Coffee and Play

A dedicated artist starts at 6 . . . 6 am, that is. "Let's make art grandpa!" With coffee in hand, I quietly walk with her down to the studio. As a supportive assistant, I listen to Danielle's well-formed plans of what she wants to do. Her ideas and her enthusiasm are plentiful. Danielle shows me her collection of hair clips. She savors all the things she bought and claims to have "the best idea ever!" "I want to make hair clip holders—one for my sister and one for me." Then, Danielle says, "We will make a store to sell it." Danielle takes the lead, describing all the things she wants to do. At this point, she scans the studio floor and the many interesting discards to collect. She also looks through the trashcans for other treasures she wants. Danielle is constantly shopping for supplies and ideas everywhere and constantly identifies objects with possibilities.

Danielle collects all the scissors in the room. She claims that scissors are her favorite things. Freely, she cuts into different materials, shaping flower forms and hearts. Danielle decorates her growing garden with stars and stickers, ribbons and buttons. Some flowers receive a cut out photo of her sister; in others, she draws pictures of her mom with a heart head. Each flower is matched with a different long, colored ribbon from which to hang the hair clips and price tags. Art comes from the heart, so she makes hearts for people she loves. But the play is also about a store, so play and art, the fanciful and utilitarian, are blended to meet her goal.

A Grand Opening

After a morning of playing and making the store's stock, Danielle declares, "It's ready!" From the laundry room she borrows a basket to stack and assemble as the shop counter. Danielle arranges the hair clip holders, adding play money and gift cards made from playing cards and cardboard pieces. On a glittery sheet of foam, she constructs an image of the store for an advertising banner, decorating each stick-on letter. High art, craft, designing, and decorating are all parts of playing. Danielle's store is an installation of play objects, decorative signs, and inventive store fixtures. The grand opening is a collaborative pretend play, a performance in which the family participates. The Hair Clip Store is Danielle's art. It is also a model for rethinking art rooms and art teaching.

Day Two (6 am or Even Earlier)

Danielle's art is made for someone special. It's dedicated to a special recipient before it's made. Her second day of artistic play is about gifts, such as the necklace with found object charms for her sister. Before starting, Danielle parades about the studio in front of me modeling a gold marker cap and a short white zipper as possible floor-picked charms. Playing before a friendly audience helps to brainstorm and formulate artistic decisions.

Later that day, after a museum visit, Danielle holds everyone's entry pins. She playfully tries them on every part of her clothing. Each pin is customized as a gift, and she describes everyone wearing it. The art to wear is carefully giftwrapped in fine paper and fabric scraps. Danielle has many suggestions for wearing and playing art and how her art in school could all be "gift wrapped presents."

Day Three (5 am . . . She Could Not Wait, Being So Excited by a New Idea)

At breakfast, Danielle has already made plans to play princess. She looks through her supply box for what she needs for the play. She picks some glittery foam to make a crown with a setting of buttons and sticker jewels. It's all art, it's all play, posing in a crown, and measuring fabric for a cape. A fancy cape it is, with stapled ribbons and cut out drawings. She asks for a royal mirror to review the royal garments. Danielle's art grows and comes alive in pretend playing. She says her art in school is "just for portfolios, refrigerator doors" and not stuff to play with or wear.

Day Four (6:30-ish)

A day after the holidays, there are plenty of great boxes, padding forms, and giftwrap to go through. The morning starts with Danielle surveying the pile prepared for recycling day. Breakfast is abbreviated due to the urgency of her desire to add to her play supplies. On this, the fourth day of her visit, Danielle used up most ribbon rolls and was left with an assortment of rolling spools to play test. Improvised spool games combined with a bounty of boxes suggest this day be dedicated to inventing wheeled toys.

Finding yellow surveyor's tape in the studio leads to her first object, the school bus. Spools are attached to a gift box and mummified with yellow tape and white stickers. On the small white sticker-canvases Danielle draws windows and portraits of the driver with happy passengers. She wants me to help cut open the box top for a sunroof and easy access for arranging play figures inside. Being a toy maker is certainly one of Danielle's favorite artistic expressions. It's almost noon, and Danielle is still focused on the school bus—adding a felt road with yellow markings and road signs before the test drive. The bus makes stops around the table during lunch with such fun that it seems school art should be renamed Toy Making 101.

Day Five (5 am)

With a day set aside for packing, Danielle wants to start making things extra early. A show is scheduled for the final day at Grandpa's house.

Chairs are moved from other parts of the house and lined up in the studio. Danielle makes an advertising poster for the show, illustrating all her play and art making. All that was made during the past few days is set up in a toy-store-like display. Before a crowd of seated dolls and family members, Danielle models her royal gown and pulls her rolling toys. Her sister models the gifts of jewelry. For the special event, she makes gift bags stuffed with original found-object art, using up most of the items collected for the week. Different from the end to a traditional art show, with critiques or bulletin board exhibits, this playful art show concludes a special art experience in a way that could be fully practiced in art class endings.

Parting Thoughts

After a holiday spent in playing with Danielle, I have a foam-glitter-sheet filled with hearts, painted with nail polish, to frame that I can proudly display on my art room door—like a certificate of graduation from "play school." My time with my granddaughter filled me with inspiration to share with my students. I go to my art class proudly wearing a crown and cape and telling vivid stories of a young artist at play. My experience curating her art and bringing examples to school helped me recognize the results of her inventive play as original art-works. From this visit, I took away lessons learned from watching her creative processes, and I was able to pass what I learned onto the students in my own art classroom.

Play and the Search for Creative Ideas

To be an independent artist requires the ability to be curious, to discover one's own art ideas. Think of play as a learner's permit that will guide children toward that discovery. It moves young artists along the open road of the imagination, helping them to experience independence, to experiment, to gather ideas, to chart a course, and to explore its boundaries and challenges. Playing in an art class builds a belief in one's own powers, abilities, and resourcefulness. It is an education in self-education, in learning to become one's own art teacher and achieve license as an independent artist who can take the lifetime art trip alone.

FIGURE 2.4 Children's art is like a transforming toy that is altered in playing.

Play demonstrates art as a search and not an assignment. Children don't need to enter into a project with a specific outcome in mind—they can experiment. In the art class, acts of play allow students to experience the 'unassigned' side of school. Raised on art assignments, students cannot function as creative people after school. For students to discover and invent ideas is the principal contribution of an art class. They can figuratively step outside of the rigid mental state school demands toward the uncontrived autonomy they exercise in home studios and self-assigned tasks. Players must be free to dream and think about what they want to do before they can do anything truly unique.

Play empowers students. When the art lesson is always a demonstration of the art teacher's ideas, students forget that they have any. To celebrate children's ideas, parents and art teachers should not overshadow them with theirs. Setting up an art class as a playground allows students to lead, to find ideas and become the artists in a class. Where else if not in an art class can students have an opportunity to envision great plans, to act on their best ideas, and take pride in accomplishing them? When students experience what it feels like to be an independent artist, they will not forget.

Play nurtures curiosity. Children are often naturally curious, impatient to discover, uncover, and experiment. Playing in an art class provides opportunities for young artists who want to try things. These are invaluable traits, considering the self-education required in making art. Patience is important but so is the willingness to tinker and explore, drawing one's own conclusions. Art teaching should thus involve breaking down limitations and boundaries to art through play experiences that involve students' curiosity to try things on their own.

Starting art classes with play opens a floodgate of possibilities. It allows for uninhibited moves and improvised actions, opportunities to try things out in real time and space. For example, after creating an innovative play scenario, building the scene and performing or pretending, students maintain a sense of fun and satisfaction which can then be applied to an art project, even one based on traditional art media. Play leaves unrestricted impressions and useful plans, "mind sketches," for making things.

Play explores and explains the art process as the artistic scuffle to find ideas. A crucial element of art teaching is explaining where art ideas may come from as young artists are sent off to search. For example, accidents can be valuable sources of ideas. "Oops! I dropped something!" can turn into "look what I created!" Spills may disturb the quiet schoolroom, but they stir scores of creative possibilities in the art classroom. Those who spill cereal, drop a glass, or kick blocks can anticipate interesting results and possibilities. Floors become blank canvases decorated by playful drips and splatters that help children see art in fresh ways. Playing "oops" during art class, pushing items off a cluttered table to see what happens, can alter their perspective. Young artists need not be upset by spills; they can learn to risk purposefully to see what happens. More importantly, they can learn to see those risks as part of the artistic process.

Play challenges students to search their surroundings, consider multiple possibilities, and try the unlikely. Instead of demonstrations of what is known, play offers opportunities for discovery, a time for adventure and exploration. For example, children can accompany adults to put out the trash with the proviso that the children can look and take from anyone's sidewalk "display." The game of looking through art room trashcans celebrates children's interest in curbside shopping. Call it treasure hunting, recycling, or repurposing—through it, students learn that artists are licensed to look everywhere and to discover ideas that are gifts wasted for others.

Play inspires artistic license. How important is it to know what an object is supposed to be used for? Play teaches that artists are magicians who can convert anything into something else. Therefore, what becomes important is to find new uses for every object. Art room chairs or art tools become space ships and riding toys by the flip of the wrist. Making substitutions can be a popular art class play in which a banana is used as a phone, a raisin is tried as a microchip, and a broom becomes a dancing partner. A favorite art room play is going to a pretend store and bringing an unusual object that's hard to identify to the cash register. Everyone holding an artistic license can offer a funny guess or suggestion.

School and Efficient Learning

School teaching tends to focus on simplifying subjects, categorizing information, and finding efficient ways to present facts. A trained teacher wants to cut all irrelevant data, to reduce clutter and distraction and be able to pose specific problems. Art teaching often cuts to the chase by presenting art as a series of efficient projects, and students settle into art routines. Classes provide students with preconceived ideas about art, as information. Children, like artists, don't think or work this way; they must figure things out for themselves, get their answers from time-consuming investigation and first-hand practice.

The creative child is less efficient than adults; he or she is not as capable of cutting out unnecessary and useless information, simplifying a problem, and skipping to questions that yield the most information. What an adult thinker can do in a few seconds takes a child much longer. However, young artists have a great advantage—in most life situations, there is so much seemingly senseless data that it's impossible to tell what questions to ask. A child is much better at taking in this kind of data, tolerating its confusion, and discerning the faint signals of promise among all the noise. But this takes time and encouragement.

Thinking for the students, or getting students to think the way adults do, seems more efficient, especially in the fast-paced school day. Art classes thus need to counteract that efficiency to nurture the kind of curiosity and creative thinking that is vital to art. Exploration may not seem immediately productive, but overall, it does yield great results not only in student confidence, motivation, and self-reliance but also in imaginative pieces of art.

Embracing the Mess

My granddaughter Danielle, when she was three, painted with her feet, and after a secret painting act you can follow her tracks around the house and find vestiges of color in her curly brown hair. For Danielle, using glue, paint, or jelly is a

FIGURE 2.5 Children make a home by moving into objects and places.

bodily act of getting into media. Granddaughter Emilie, at seven, mixed colors with any tool she could find and used her necklace of porcelain doll hands for stirring and to spread her newly discovered colors into paintings. Many of these found brushes were stuck onto the painting and became part of her final art.

In brief, I have addressed the importance of patience regarding children's so-called mess and junk. In this section, I elaborate on the idea that art teaching is not about just tolerating but aiding and celebrating a child's discovery of messy art acts because those acts are innovations. Young artists often like to feel their way through the art process with open hands, submerging themselves in colors, mud, frosting, or water. Being messy is just part of a need for close contact with different substances, for creative experiments that involve learning through chaos. This may not be an aspect of every home or school art, but the messy arts are an integral part of children's art. Thus, art teachers benefit from studying children's messy art play outside of class.

Can a Mess Really Lead to Art?

Is messiness, being free to be messy and experiment with media, all that important for children? Some experienced instructors maintain that if kids are just allowed to play freely with paints or other substances, they just mix colors together without thinking about what it means, or they end up with sticky goo that can't be used for any real purpose. These instructors assume that because children are inexperienced, they just end up with mud-colored messes that aren't good for anything.

Playing, even if only to make mud, is neither a waste of paint nor a sign of an artist in need of instruction. Messing with sand, food, or paints without guilt is an important, perhaps a once-in-a-lifetime experience for children to journey to the end of colors and textures. It is the initiation to the love of mixing and spontaneously dispersing all media. It is a journey that cannot be taken through color charts or neatly charted exercises. Messing with colors and textures, in any substance, teaches a lesson about the sense of joy in discovery, in play, in engaging physical senses, and in continuing until the creative expression emerges, even if that expression looks like nothing more than a mud puddle. There are possibilities in that puddle that only the artist can imagine.

Resisting Fear

Adults tend to see themselves as guardians against mess whose job is to prevent children from starting a mess or to be there with a towel to minimize it. Adults often offer ample praise for children who stay in line, clean their hands, and wipe their feet. This coaches the young toward a culture of order and an aesthetic of neatness. In some cases at home, children are allowed a modicum of messiness when they are young, but this generally doesn't last long after they are considered able to clean up after themselves. By the time children enter school, the tendency toward messiness is expected to be gone since it has no place in a classroom.

Such fears about making a mess can prevent an important aspect of artistic play for children. Rushing children to wash their hands whenever they submerge them in new substances clearly states, "be careful and not playful." Restricting play to only a small area of the house or even the outdoors to avoid messes restricts their imagination. But there's a thrill in leaving stains, in not mopping up a spill just to see the pattern it makes, that encourages experimentation and even teaches about ways to calculate a mess for an artistic purpose. Children can develop a lifetime of art ideas from the messes they are able to make as children, if the adults who guide them can be released from their fears of the mess. It just takes time, patience, and a little planning.

Preparing for the Mess

Designing a classroom for art inspiration involves setting up creative play spaces that allow for messy creative acts. It also involves providing varied cover-ups, surfaces, tools, and mediums to encourage the drippy experimenter. Children can feel welcome to play messy in a sea of drop cloth covering the floor and nice furniture. Giving them aprons or dressing them in plastic suits to play in the kitchen or an art room also frees them from worrying. Young artists cannot drip or bounce paint-soaked squish balls or sail painted butterfly wings when worried about where marks might land. However, when teachers cover prohibited surfaces, there is no fear of hitting the edges where art ends and school begins. Innovation and free movement reign with every dip, drip, or bounce of flowing colors.

If circumstances forbid drop cloth coverings, another way to escape the proverbial box in art innovation is for students to get messy in boxes. Flat boxes, trays, even play pools allow for working in a tub-like container that is similar to the freedoms a bathtub provides for free water playing. Inside a pizza box, for example, there is room for stirring paints and mixing toppings. Painting trays, baking tins, or cookie sheets are useful for play with glue, glitter, or flowing paint. Take-home restaurant containers provide children a place to make a mess and not worry about drying time because they have easy closures for transport.

Of course, an art room well-stocked with a variety of non-traditional objects and finds provided by the teacher and students already includes the tools for messy art play, whether they are sticks, stones, toothbrushes, doll hands, tires, flippers, or any number of objects. Just like each object changes the possibilities of the art, so do the different types of coverings used for the messy work: for example, paper tablecloths soak up paint, while plastic repels it. Fur or carpet pieces can be both a paint brush and a canvas. The more choices, the more swishing, swashing, marking, messy fun opportunities for art.

From Messy Playing to Art

Just as children test their bodies in free dancing and outrageous choreography, freely moving and being messy with media are basic art dances. Experiencing painting can be mixing colors by hand, or painting with the paint jars lid. Working in surprising ways, doing the unexpected and even the unacceptable occasionally is part of a journey into new ways of experiencing art making. Children constantly find ways to move messy playing into new art forms.

For art teaching, it is important to witness children's many self-initiated art-making acts, to learn about children's handling of materials. Art teachers need to step back to appreciate children's ways of doing things. Through pouring, spilling, dropping, and other "illogical" experiments, students uncover their own paths to making art. Children who are not allowed to squeeze out their own toothpaste, to stick their hands in a jar of glue, or to pick paint without having it doled out to them, miss an opportunity for developing self-sufficiency as artists. This doesn't mean that art teachers need to encourage a free-for-all mess fest. Sometimes, all that's required is to take bits and pieces of messy acts and skillfully apply them to classroom situations.

If art for children is truly about process and not the product, messy playing is an essential means to experience aspects of the process. In messy play, students feel safe to explore the imperfect side of art and creation. Untidy media play promotes experiences with the accidental and chaotic, and this is an important way that artists uncover new avenues for creating.

Creative Play Themes

Classic themes in adult art—the figure, landscape, and still life—are also important themes in play. In fact, the classic themes merge in children's play experiences. Playing with scores of figures before they draw or paint figures, children build, dress, pose, and animate toys. Before they ever sketch a landscape, children play in dirt; they play with water, leaves, and nature's discards. Through setting tables, arranging the refrigerator, or creatively designing object arrangements from Mom's old jewelry box, they organize still life scenes. As children rehearse themes in their play, as they explore the new from the old, they actually achieve major innovations and take traditional art categories into new realms of contemporary art. Here is an overview of a few general play themes that act out different scenarios. See chapter six for more detailed examples of more specific play themes to integrate in the play-based art classroom.

Example Play Themes

Play art can be observed in children's **scenario play**, as when children play school or play house. They use their classroom experiences to create their own school scenarios, imagine different types of education settings and experiences.

They recreate domestic scenes and spaces by climbing into boxes, moving under a table or bed, creating a blanket fort, or furnishing a closet house. Young architects, interior designers, and future homeowners rehearse using non-traditional bricks of books and pillows. Creating scenarios inspires a sense of design, of organization, of varied interests.

Meal play allows children to use everything they can find at home to create foods and restaurants for play figures. Children's play art is the design of unusual tables and fancy, unexpected table settings for mealtime. Even what the children use as food emerges from creative thought. This original art requires no cookbooks with glossy photos, no blueprints—just a fresh infusion of imagination.

Play art also happens in **party play**—not the ones parents organize, but parties that children invent and manage with household objects and play figures. In an art class, students never tire of recasting favorite birthday or tea party ideas. Such play has multidimensional components, from handmade invitations and birthday wrapping, to freestyle cake building. A party play can include multiple contemporary art forms melded by the vision of a young party planner.

Play art can certainly include opening up a countless number of different stores. **Store play** consists of stock found indoors or in a backyard, set up as ingenious aisles of displays. Children can create unusual boxes and price tags, ties, shopping bags, or other consumer goods as play store displays. Any art room can display a "Space to Lease" sign and host a grocery store, post office, bank, or bakery.

Dress up is a form of play art that makes any moment a special occasion. To watch children getting ready each morning is to see them play. They can dress play figures or willing pets with their own designs and collections. Just about any object, a pencil or plastic fork, can become a mannequin or model for young designers. Family closets are costume troves for the fashion conscious eye. Whether they are dressed in leaves or adding-machine tape, for children there is always time for another fashion show. Art classes for all grades need to continue this open view of wearable art and showcase new lines of impromptu creations.

In **construction play** at home, children use everything from ice cubes to play blocks and build structures. An accessible Tupperware drawer allows a city to rise. An open cupboard licenses a monumental tower of Pringles. From the smallest sugar packets at a restaurant, to pillow sculptures at home, children turn everything into building blocks. Daring gravity, children balance skyscrapers, span bridges across beds, and erect a stadium dome from a laundry basket anchored by books. There is no shortage of construction kits in any art class equipped with erasers, rulers, or pencils and, on a rainy day, plenty of umbrellas.

After children invent new constructions, they often take pleasure in demolishing what they built. This **take-apart play** clears the canvas and satisfies the curiosity over chaos. Taking objects apart also fulfills a desire to see what's inside everything, to figure out how things work, and children delight in using a hammer or screwdriver to enter an object. Given the right toolbox, a student can turn an old rotary phone into an adventure in destruction.

Transformation play occurs when children treat the objects around them like transformer toys. This play art demonstrates the magic of an imagination that is able to provide found objects with new identities and take any form and use it in new ways. Transformer artists can pretend and remodel. School art can be conducted via plays that show the infinite lives and possibilities in ordinary objects.

After learning to crawl and walk, children can invent **movement and dance play**. Rehearsals for original skating spins and high-flying snowboarding leaps are types of movement play. Playing with hula hoops, riding stick horses, or test-driving a pogo stick in the art room wakes up silent bodies, turning them into choreographers for play figures and movement inventors for paintbrushes.

Children are the directors, set designers, costumers, and **performance artists** in the many shows they produce. "Let's make a show," can precede the rise of a towel or blanket as curtains or backdrops for dancing jugglers or stuffed animals used in magic acts. Children parade about in tutus and sunglasses playing Geppetto, animating and channeling their voices through teddy bears.

In **invention play**, a child playfully stages and supervises the count down and blast of a yellow pencil seated on top of a banana. They narrate and track the pencil's planetary journey on a smartphone. Inventors of robots working on conveyor belts to create instant donuts and other discoveries emanate from children's play ventures that penetrate the possibilities of objects and imagine the future. When home laboratories are closed down, innovative ideas need to be sustained and cultivated by art room play.

What Play-Based Art Teachers Do

Even though students play an important role in preparing for each art class, play-based art teachers are far from unemployed. Their 'To Do List' is vast, but it is also ideally creative and fun. Over coffee, other art teachers shared their insights about preparing their play-based classes. They focus on what the room will look like, dressing up to play roles, providing objects, and encouraging excitement with the unexpected. Overall, they agree that it's about inspiring fantasies.

The insights of these play-based art teachers also included instructive stories of playing memorable parts. As one stated, "As an art teacher I feel creative, childlike, and playful, ready to inspire others to play and create." As the children enter the magical place called an art room, it's up to them to look around and be inspired by the environment created by the teacher in order to find things and playfully create. One art teacher's list of roles included shopkeeper, moving man, magician, set or interior designer, and of course artist.

As important as creating fantasies and practicing many supportive roles is for the play-based art teacher, it's just as important to playfully demonstrate and rehearse creative behaviors with students. For example, walking the runway of the center of the art room, an art teacher can model a shiny pot cover hat before passing it on to a student who then conjures a car, makes a right hand turn, signaling with his hands, blowing the horn, and turning the pot cover steering wheel. When the next student takes charge, the pot cover is a drum, used to perform a solo jazz set. The play is so much fun that the art teacher joins in, picking up a badminton racquet to use as a guitar for accompaniment. Using acting, performance, sound effects, and the space of the room, players can be guided by the teacher to explore the many lives of ordinary objects.

As one play-based art teacher reflects,

> It's important that I play before the children, and I play with them. I act as a cheerleader for great ideas, an older playmate, a partner, a fellow artist, or assistant that helps students realize what they are trying to do. I may share a few of my ideas, but it's like the objects in the room, some notice, others ignore it. That's great because students don't see me as the boss or director of their art. They know me as someone who gets excited about fine thoughts and is always ready to listen and help.

Essentially, play-based art teachers work towards inciting the imagination and building confidence in their students' creative actions and ideas. Teachers organize play to encourage student discoveries, to engage student hands and resourcefulness. Trying out and play-testing everything to uncover possibilities is what the artist-as-teacher does to embolden the student-as-artist.

While chapter seven addresses more teacher recommendations in detail, here I offer a quick outline of how to prepare the art classroom as an encouraging, creative environment that will establish some basis for thinking about the play chapters that follow. Each day, a play-based art teacher:

- Creates challenging stories to lead a classroom adventure.
- Plans and executes a new classroom setting to inspire players' fantasies.
- Models playing before the class and joins in student play.
- Ensures that students have room and time to play before and during art project work.
- Plans for an active play start to an art lesson.
- Makes certain that there are blocks, teddy bears, fast food figures, and other interesting found objects to play with in the room.
- Challenges students to bring objects and ideas to class, to show and tell, and prepares students to leave the room with plans and ideas beyond the art period.

- Sets up for explorations and surprises, things to build, to take apart, things to puzzle over, to think about.
- Assembles intellectual appetizers; conversation starters; tickets to imaginative journeys; things to touch, try out, try on, hold, examine, look at, and admire.
- Uses proclamations to start the play: "let the play begin," "let's pretend," "let's make believe," "let's make up a story."
- Provides for the unexpected: taking off shoes, getting messy, painting with water and mops on the floor, opening a surprise package.
- Promotes a grand finale, a final show, performance, or parade, to introduce the toys and celebrate the art made in class.

3

A CLASSROOM ENVIRONMENT FOR PLAY AND ART

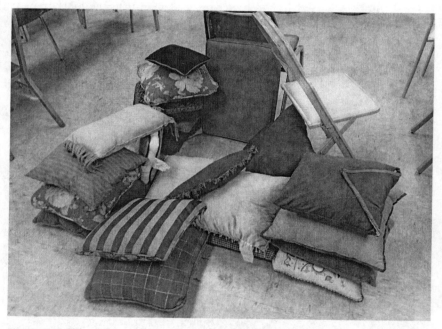

FIGURE 3.0 When the world is viewed as the largest art supply store, anything can be the material or tool for making art.

This chapter compares the child's studio at home and the typical art room. It explores the elements within those rooms that set the stage for curiosity and motivation to join in creative playing. The creation of fantasy and adventure settings focuses on visual surroundings that provide multisensory clues that call for physical and imaginative responses.

The chapter recommends that art teachers give as much consideration to planning the art room space as they do to their lesson planning. They should use their creative insight and experiences to create art classroom "playscapes" favorable to play that adapt the elements of, for example, playing outdoors at the beach, in parks, and backyards, and playing indoors in children's rooms, the porch, kitchen, or bathtub. A different kind of lesson planning is emphasized that draws on fantasy settings, playful material displays, and small but significant room changes to promote a variety of artistic and imaginative uses.

Classroom Environments for Play

For the past 40 years, I have demonstrated the art of creative art teaching at conventions, museums, and universities. It is has always been difficult to predict the appearance of each ballroom, the qualities of theaters, or the contents of lecture halls. Everything had to be set up to demonstrate the look of an art room that invites playing.

In the past, it was easy to fly and take along the contents of a room to set up anywhere. Like an archeologist, I would pack up my children's supplies and inventions in carefully numbered boxes and set up their play as it was set up in their "messy room." To the Lyndon B. Johnson Library, I even took a separate suitcase just for the surplus parachute my children re-configured into magical domes to create many different play spaces. The audience sat under this cloud of floating white silk as they listened about art and play.

FIGURE 3.1 In play and art, anything can be a canvas.

Today's airline restrictions have grounded my habit of borrowing props from children's rooms. Yet, I still travel extensively to demonstrate art rooms as play environments, centers for children's creativity and innovation. To replicate the feel of children's rooms, now I have to depend on finding the elements for staging my theme at each site. In some ways, the later presentations have become more challenging but also more realistic in their demonstration of how children creatively borrow from their environment, how they scavenge and hunt for stuff to transform into amazing play set-ups. School art rooms should strive to promote invention by replicating the spirit that children use in setting up imaginative play environments.

The Hyatt Ballroom in Atlanta

A recent convention presentation began in silence, with the audience watching me contemplate the objects in the ballroom before I started gathering a few choices to move from their existing location to the stage.

First, I appropriated all styles of trashcans, starting in the back of the room and stacking them in the front. Removing large white tablecloths from refreshment tables took a little time, but freeing the linen canvases was worth the effort. Attractive silver ice cube bucket covers were definitely a "yes," as well as a coat hanger on wheels that happened to be in the room. I took possession of interesting stools and unusual chairs, and rolled up a piece of oriental style carpet from the entrance.

The stage became loosely filled with objects that seemed randomly positioned but which were really treasures that would yield creative ideas.

The presentation included a magic carpet ride and a blastoff from a space station of repositioned trashcans. Combined with interlocking padded chairs, the trashcans also served as wheels for a racecar during another part of the play. There was great excitement when I took control of the shiny silver steering wheel and fastened the matching hubcaps before "revving up" the engine. The white tablecloths played many roles: clouds, a full cape, and a sidewalk cafe with an awning—when combined with chairs and the rolling garment rack. The object transformations were tied together by my lecture, which mimicked the way that children talk and narrate the progress of their play.

Envisioning an Art Room Is a Creative Act

The art room as a canvas can be set up to look and feel like any place or any event. To design art rooms for playful discoveries is a daily creative challenge. In creating fantasy environments, there should be no self-imposed limits that assume something should or should not be done simply because the space happens to be in a school or in a classroom. Conjuring up amazing ideas by simple alterations of spaces and furnishing, light and sounds, introduces the unexpected and promotes fun and magic to start each class.

Designing art rooms for discovery is a challenge of creating a place that belongs to everyone. Every artist needs to feel in charge of his or her space or canvas. The room needs to be a place where it's easy to move things around and make changes, to get under things, to use the floor, to hide, and to seek. It should be a safe place to pretend in, where students feel free to use their imagination as they search for things to use, things to do, as they improvise with the room and its contents.

Ultimately, the art room should be a stress free fun-zone, a place created to look and feel unlike the rest of school. This means designing the room as an open, inviting, and less restrictive environment. Even though in a school, the art room can feel like a fun place, a birthday palace, or a secret garden where play and art are discovered.

Lessons From Home Studios

Thumping rhythms come from Emilie's room during the late hours of a sleepover. Opening the door a crack reveals children galloping in the dark on stick horses. Flashlights illuminate their path. An automated bubble blower fills the room

FIGURE 3.2 The future is modeled in the present in children's play constructions.

with bubbles. Basking in the bubbles, popping bubbles on their noses, children use the flashlights to project bubble images on walls and ceiling. Only whimsy and nonsensical pleasure direct their play. I rush for the phone to take pictures that will help set the scene for my morning art class, taking inspiration from their creativity.

Parents—Clear the Canvas

Some parents are overly concerned with decorating a child's room. However, allowing the space to function as an open and ever-changing playground for the child makes it a space of creative possibility. If walls are not freshly painted and off-limits and there is a sturdy step stool (for older children) to reach the ceiling, every surface is accessible for play use, for the child to decorate. The floor can also be a canvas if not overly cluttered and if there is no delicate or nice furniture that children can't move around. Open shelves and corners also provide possibilities for the imagination to build. And if children can import items from outside the room, they have constant opportunities to inspire new play art creations.

Teachers—Follow Suit

An art teacher is not the art room's decorator but someone who optimizes play space and usable surfaces. Permanent room markings, such as a jungle mural painted on the ceiling with matching chairs, sends a message that the space is off-limits. Access to prime wall and window play spaces can be guarded or barricaded by file cabinets, or drying racks. Some art rooms seem like holding pens, discouraging playful use of all the room's surfaces by keeping students hostage to large tables surrounded by filled shelves. However, cleaning walls and bulletin boards, taking off old posters, signs, or student art, and keeping permanent furniture or decorations to a minimum makes the art room adaptable. The following observations of home studios are important areas of appreciation for parents and learning for art teachers seeking to promote creativity.

Walls

Many museums have freed up walls from permanent hangings to allow artists to directly play on the wall. The constantly changing walls of a child's room documents recent plays and suggests many possibilities for the use of walls. Art classes can also open up walls to become communal playgrounds. With plastic covers, Lego panels, temporary wallpapers, chalkboard paints, reflective screens, students can be invited to use shadows or push pins to play on the wall.

Windows

A window is a large light box in a child's room. Plastic spider nets made from clear tape or fishing line, colorful plastic gems play with the passing light. Saran Wrap sticks like glue to shiny surfaces, allowing players a new way to see the world or a new canvas to mark up. Lining Emilie's windowsill are clear boxes, acrylic cups and bowls filled with sparkly stones. Objects on and around the window throw their reflections of colors and shadows onto interior surfaces. If the art room is lucky enough to have a window, making it accessible for use by experienced window artists pays huge dividends. Opening classroom windows to views and sounds outside the classroom and to let in the changing light can inspire play art innovations.

Ceilings

In a child's room, there is often stuff draped and spinning around the fan or hanging from the ceiling because even ceilings provide an art canvas. It can be a place to design a trapeze act or clothesline pulleys for a cable car/ski lift. Who knows what will hang or dare to walk across the high wires extended from the curtain rod to a standing lamp? Classroom ceilings can also provide a large play area with possibilities. Built-in ceiling light boxes and flexible soft grid panels can be decorated and modified, with supervision. Encouraging ceiling play is as simple as providing a set of sturdy steps and some strings, wires, springs, netting, pins, or Velcro.

Shelves, Boxes, and Counters

Children constantly enrich their spaces by saving interesting objects they've picked up and displaying them on shelves or in open drawers. Three-dimensional dioramas live on dresser tops and share a showcase with innovative fashion, modeled by a teddy bear. The lid of a closed toy box becomes an exercise studio on the penthouse level of an urban condo. A tall shoe rack in a child's closet becomes a doll jungle gym. Counters with sinks become pools. Spaces that offer fun at home also play well in school. All the available drawers and shelves children use at home can be made welcome play spaces in an art room.

Lighting

To be in control of one's creative space requires being in charge of the lights. Children like to play with light switches, thus learning about space and how it changes by lighting. Creating light shows is one of children's favorite nighttime activities. Darkness is exciting and much play takes place with flashlights, nightlights, and portable lamps. Standing on a stool with a flashlight, a child can direct a circus of toy figures in a rink made from bike reflectors. Performers become giants, enlarged as shadows all over the room.

Setting up an art room involves building an interesting flashlight collection. Scout out signal lights with color filters, miner's safety lights, or new and antique flashlights; each has its own warmth, coolness, and special glow. The art room can be set up as a place to manipulate and modify lights, to play with vintage projectors, star machines, dimmers, and filtering devices. The space can become a planetarium, a rock stage, with light shows displayed on the big screen of the classroom wall or ceiling.

Sound

Each time someone enters Emilie's room, a potted singing and dancing flower performs "You Are My Sunshine." Emilie has an infinite repertoire of dance improvisations this song inspires. Sounds from television commercials, toy instruments, and iPod speakers spur children's playful movements and provide new ideas for dances and play with toys and art tools. Soundtracks can turn a play into a musical with dancing figures or tools.

In an art class set up for songs and dancing, students come alive and freely move with objects and tools. Active music makers, not passive listeners, promote playful moves. Equipping an art room for sound doesn't require having the highest quality Bose speakers. Students learn to make their own instruments and find sounds and sound-making devices. They create their own band or orchestra with sticks, trashcans, strumming combs, and hotel bells. Musical toys, folk instruments, synthesizers, party noise makers, or child-sized grand pianos from secondhand stores can lead a parade, accompany a toy performance, or enliven a play fashion show. A big drum can be ready and set up to lead a hallway parade of pull toys.

A Little Effort, a Lot of Reward

Promoting play in an art room takes a conscious and consistent effort to maintain open access to all of the room's potential canvases. Both parents and teachers can design rooms not just to showcase children's art but also to inspire artistic creativity. All designs should welcome alterations that allow as many spaces and surfaces as possible to be used in playing. When children have control over their spaces, they have the freedom to reach new imaginative heights.

Children's Rooms Set Up for Play

Children's play and art can be best observed in home studios because the areas where they play at home tend to best represent their freest experimentations. Such observations are invaluable for envisioning changes to the school art room that will inspire creative players. Here are some aspects of children's rooms and home studios that can be replicated in the art room.

3D Play

A Barbie aerobics class set up on a blanket on the floor reflects the kind of three-dimensional constructions of action play models with settings and scenery that dominate most children's rooms. To allow for some of the same 3D plays in the art class, school furnishings need to be movable, providing easy access to set up on the floor. A collection of interesting items, including blankets, carpet pieces, unusual drop cloths, or sections of foam can serve as underlays on which children can set up a picnic with teddy bears, take a magic carpet ride, or set up aerobics and other settings with play figures.

Disorganization

When playing, children conveniently spread out into any available space, and as their ideas develop the amount of space they take up can extend. Also the space in a child's room tends to be populated with the chaos of multiple temporary play constructions and by toys. This may make their areas seem disorganized and messy, but it's a creative mess.

That is why the art class needs enough room for children to create play settings and be surrounded by interesting objects, whether collected on site or imported to class. Not only the floor but also the room needs to be open for free arranging. Art rooms can be unbound from stable furniture and become mobile. Formal seating plans can give way to students moving ideas and activities that can cross the room. It may look like chaos, but in fact, each player creates his or her own play space and has a creative plan and idea for organization.

Can art teachers in school let go of the natural inclination to clean up all disorder? As I explained in chapter two, creating a classroom environment for play requires setting up a mental attitude of tolerance and a program for educating other adults who may enter the room. A sign outside the door may look like a construction site warning: *Artists At Work*. An art room organized with neat storage bins and containers all filled with the same art supplies to hand out to everyone is not as conducive to inspiring varied play and the unique art that comes from that play. After all, welcoming students' own treasures, street finds, and collections and respecting their imaginative endeavors leads to objects and art pieces that are not easily taken down, stored, or put into pre-labeled storage containers. An art room should look as messy and complex as the child's room to foster a diversity of activities and house a variety of objects and materials that will encourage play.

Hiding Places

At home, we don't always know where the young artist can be found. She may be setting up school in her closet or preparing a domed baseball stadium under the bed. Children create their own undercover worlds under blankets or use their towels to drape chairs and spaces between furnishings. Play settings in boxes, covered cabanas, and secret dwellings appear as a complex web of rooms within the larger room. The very act of finding or creating a suitable hiding space and using that space to develop play is a creative endeavor. However, at school, everybody is in sight and accounted for. Areas are not set up to be interesting or to provide good hiding spaces; they are meant to ensure everyone can be seen and assessed while they engage in designated actions.

In a stroll through the art room, students can take stock and point out the possibilities for spaces they would like to play in. An art room that provides places they can call their own for a short time and safe places to hide offers a variety of play opportunities. The point in creating space is simply to give children the room to work as they need, whether they seek to be undercover or simply find a shelf on which to create an imaginative setting. For undercover plays to continue, the art room can provide fabrics, blankets, or saved drapery to create 'bubbles,' domes, or tents. Towels can be available to drape over chairs and space under tables made accessible. Corners are cherished by students and need to be cleared for use. Cabinets can provide opening stages for play. Art room racks, carts, and shelves are valuable properties to be leased to the player's imagination. Children who have a long-standing love of opening kitchen drawers and cabinets know exactly what to do when the doors to these small rooms are reopened. The key is to provide everything from furniture to building materials to offer a creative haven for invention.

Openness & Variety

Play set-ups with boxes and figures can be small and privately played out on the seat of a chair. Another play scenario like a candy store may use all the chairs and candy stashes in a child's room. An art room set-up for players has to make allowances for a variety of intentions, so each student can make changes and playfully use furnishings to organize the space. To easily move in an art room, students need to take ownership of the space, to locate what they need and want to use. A stack of identical papers placed on identical art tables with identical pens or paints fence out possibilities and bind everyone to similar acts and similar work. Art rooms need open space and a feeling of being able to spread out and spread the wings of imagination to fly off the table and set up under it.

Exploration

Adults often have difficulty understanding child's play—the children involved must demonstrate how it works, what's happening, and offer their personal creative visions to explain and complete the piece. Also, in children's rooms, they are in charge. They set their own creative goals; they decide what to use, when to start or take a break, whom to include, and when a play is over. Playing in their space, they learn to steer and make artistic decisions, to test and follow creative intuitions. A child's studio is thus an active workspace that allows taking out and using all kinds of stuff that offers possibilities.

Maybe this is why it's easier for many adults to lead art class in a uniform way, so they can understand what everyone does. They provide an example of the work and have all the students replicate it. However, an art room set-up for players should not be an assembly line that reigns in playful art possibilities. The art room, like the child's room, is for incubating ideas, ambiguous and mysterious creations in progress, and inventions in flux. The playroom needs to be a setting where things can be temporarily set up to be explored and ideas altered or rebuilt by players. A different kind of art teaching does not focus on controlling the meaning or production of children's art. Art teachers should encourage by admiring at a distance, without posing as experts and offering advice and criticism. Let the students unveil their explorations and explain in their own time and in their own way.

Props & Wardrobe

A child's room is a stage that goes through many scene changes. During one play, it can be a robot's lab, in another, an operating room, test kitchen, or a mad scientist's laboratory. Each name signifies a different attitude towards the room and the experiments booming inside. Each play signifies a different approach to the props and wardrobe needed to accompany the scene. For example, in a color lab for inventing new colors, a rolling tool chest with mixing bowls, a blender, wooden spoons, and plastic trays provides places to safely mix and pour colors. Such a messy endeavor also may require children to wear gloves, robes, facemasks, goggles, or hard hats. Protecting the room from the color mixing may require lots of drop cloths and protective coverings that allow moving off one play-spot. Looking outside the typical art room toolbox means giving students leeway and also providing some of the more practical considerations that they might not include to set the stage for creativity.

Partnering

Children often ask adults to play house or urge friends to join in their building dreams. Friends become partners in playing store, restaurant, or setting up a stadium in a child's sizeable dresser drawer. Partnering can include being a team of two individual players, members of a cast, or a performer and audience. When children play with partners, there is a new excitement and boost of energy for their creative playing. But it's important to let the children choose the partners they want to include in their exhibitions and performances. Rather than using assigned seating in art rooms, keep the space open for new partnerships. Try to provide room for individual, team, or ensemble play. A play-based classroom benefits from a set-up where students can join creative teams and other inventors.

The Doors to Art

Finding a child's room is easy; just look for the handsome display of art on the door. Items ranging from handmade signs and doorknob hangings to Post-it drawings and souvenirs populate the rotating door exhibit. For the full effect, one needs to film the development of a door over a period of time. The playful use of the frame and door panels is a preview to attractions inside. Once you find the door, you get a glimpse of the artist's many interests and style.

Children's art experience all starts at the door, where they can immediately recognize the difference between an art room set up for learning how to

FIGURE 3.3 In a busy world, creative ideas are often framed in privacy under a table.

draw or paint and one where they will play. An interesting doorway to the art room serves as an exciting entrance into an imaginative world. It's an introduction to creativity, a showcase, yet another space of possibility that tickles the fancy. That is why setting up an art room for playing starts at the door. Since every art classroom is filled with qualified designers and decorators with door-art experience, why not offer the art room door to the young artists within? Have a handy tape dispenser nearby and invite students to turn an ordinary schoolroom entrance into a lively marquee promoting the playful acts inside.

Welcome!

Some parents see a child's decorated door and think it must be dangerous to enter. The door is booby-trapped! It's so messy, you'll fall and trip inside. But when children enter the same door exhibiting creative designs, they see a sign that says, "Welcome to play!" The art class door can be a daily menu for the surprises and creative staging in the room. Offered as a fancy-free surface open to change, the entrance prepares and exercises the play spirit of waiting students.

Examples

Door decorations can change depending on the day or the students' desires. There can be temporary signs that welcome you to Lego Land or large footprints on the floor that indicate the start of a prehistoric passage. The entrance can be a door to a castle or the hatch to the space shuttle. Or, there may be a red carpet rolled out for a star to enter a fancy gala.

Think of the doorframe as a large picture frame that can be constantly decorated. One day, it may wear an assortment of bright tapes, another day a collection of candy wrappers. The door itself is a mannequin that can be dressed in endless covers like fur, an unusual strip of wallpaper, or reflective foil. The door can also be a picture gallery, showing previews of creations by previous dwellers.

The door doesn't have to just lead to adventures; it can be its own adventure. It can be a curtain—such as a crumpled brown paper connecting to other crumpled papers that connect to tables posing as caves to crawl into inside. Block the door so anyone who enters must remove an obstacle. Seal it by paper or plastic to be punctured and crawled through. Make peepholes or large openings to crawl inside. Create a geometry of tape or find an opening in a weaving that feels like a spider's net. Turn the door into a musical instrument played by the bodies crossing thresholds of noisy hanging beads and chains. Use a fan to create a wind tunnel or act as a prelude to the magic carpet flights about to take off inside.

Entrances

Art teachers can take the opportunity for entrances to set classroom scenes and play fun roles. They can be waiters, ushers, or friendly tour guides, even providing a menu, itinerary, or some other introduction to what's to be expected in the room. They can give the students shopping bags and special hats to introduce them to the day. Standing at the door is a creative act, and the opening or overture to the art inside. By being there when the students enter, teachers signal to students to come in and join the fun.

Floors

My future art teachers are still talking about the time we crawled behind my granddaughter Aliza, who was then one year old, to appreciate her sense of wonder about objects on the ground. We all watched her meticulously investigate and even taste interesting finds from this perfect exploring position. Crawling Aliza was a human vacuum, picking up all kinds of things. She patiently surveyed all that was new on the floor and bulldozed any obstacle that got in the way of what she wanted. With an innate GPS, Aliza zoomed towards enticing faraway objects to pick up and handle. She took stock of everything on the floor and charted their co-ordinates so she could return to what she wanted to try again. Some things she sat to play with a long time, others she appreciated with a single touch. Her exploration showed us that playing with forms and using them creatively work together.

Learning to walk placed a distance between Aliza and the objects she investigated on the floor. Growing up places an even larger distance between touching, handling, and experimenting with ground finds. Adults often don't take the time or make an effort to look down, to bend down for the seemingly insignificant. There is generally little encouragement for older kids to be on the floor as a creative way to spend time or to look down and pick up stuff for pleasure. However, this is what many contemporary artists do.

Jackson Pollock moved his painting to the floor, and the art world has never been the same. He used sticks to coax colors out of cans. His sticks were magic wands, which allowed his movements over the canvas on the floor to be playfully recorded. The floor opened up Pollock's ability to move with paint in ways that had not been done before.

Every art teacher should be delighted if their students have Aliza's patience and dedication to the study of forms. Is it too late to move art classes back to the floor? Would students of all ages benefit as creative individuals, seekers, and inventors if they had more time to spend as treasure seekers on art room (and outside) large-scale floor canvases? There are great benefits to playing with figures, blocks, found forms, and even traditional paints on the floor. Art teachers of students of all ages can move to the floor to where play began to reinvent art. Essentially, everybody needs to get down to play.

Setting Up and Playing on Floors

When was the last time you looked down and really got close to the floor, just for the pleasures of exploring? You may have lost something on the floor and had to look, but did you really get involved with the fascinating object world below? Moving attention away from desks to the floor demonstrates art to be about playful acts on any surface. While young children naturally gravitate to the floor, in a school setting with older students, the art teacher needs to pave the way. Art teachers need to be seen taking off their shoes, crawling, kneeling, or sitting on the floor when students enter.

When the art teacher is comfortable on the floor, she or he welcomes players to an informal, exploratory, and imaginative play world that does not exist any-where in a school. When the art teacher is on the floor, students of all ages feel free to get down and try it. New relationships between students and the teacher take place on the floor. There is a sense of closeness and camaraderie, a freedom to play and explore akin to playing in children's rooms at home.

Floor art can begin with the teacher getting down on the floor with students to look for, move, and arrange anything that may have landed on the floor. Or the art teacher can create different floor settings that encourage play on the floor. For example, turning the floor into a beach with a play pool and towels. Later, rain may follow (a mysterious squirt of water), forcing everyone to crawl under the shelter of desks. Seeing the art teacher play on the floor like this sends a message to students of all ages to join in inventions. It also underscores that floor play is not just for young children.

As the art teacher repeatedly alters the floor, students begin to look not to the board for assignments but down under their feet for surprises and clues. Demonstrating the uninhibited use of a room's largest canvas opens the way for students to chime in—to playfully respond with ideas and suggestions.

Starting Floor Play

The floors suggest a sense of open borders, seeing in the distance, hovering at different eye levels to see in new ways. Bigger than a shoebox, or any other canvas in class, floors can be paved in a variety of ways to suggest paths, roads, runways, or distant freeways. Floors can be set up as a test-track for toys or parading play figures. Different covers, draping, and overlays can alter the feel of the floor. Painting or building over dirt, grass, or the school desk is an entirely different experience. Art room floors can be easily changed, re-dressed, marked with signs, mapped with objects to make a large impact and suggest an infinite variety of play responses.

Spaces and floor shapes can be defined with tape or a variety of physical dividers. Spaces can be partitioned with runners or set up with random tiles. Single objects can mark individual play areas, or the space can be opened as a communal playground for group work. Young children or adults can find respite on individual tiles, or suitcase studios, or work in design teams.

Setting up for a picnic outdoors is a logical introduction to creating on the floor. For younger children, it may be designs for an outing with stuffed animals, while older students may be thinking of a still life on the grass. Playing on outdoor floors can involve collecting natural building materials from pine needles to pine cones, or bringing tile collections, pavers, surveyor's ribbons, and flags.

Floor Plays for All Ages

Students of all ages need to return to such basics of art as Aliza's love of seeking out forms and exploring shapes on the floor. Such a fascination with forms and shapes does not vanish; it can quickly be rekindled with interesting floor play in indoor or outdoor art sessions. The longer students have been away from floor plays, the more surprising and fun it is. Playing on the floor changes everyone's spirit, their relationship to the art teacher, and their notion of art. Moving desks aside is like moving aside the rigid expectations of what can be done in school and in art and starting fresh.

Chairs

At home, chairs are used as a favorite play-prop. They are dressed and draped to play different roles. Chairs are used to build instant scenery and hiding places. Dining room chairs serve as armatures, mannequins, easels, tunnels, or cars to get-up-and-go. Demonstrated to be an instant art supply, chairs are some of the most available and flexible transformer toys children use. However, they are seldom set up to invite inspiration or to be a part of the creative action in an art classroom.

Since children unreservedly use chairs at home for playing, parents and teachers need to make allowances for and nurture these imaginative architecture and design experiences. Rather than keeping a uniform set of chairs in silent rows, have an interesting variety of chairs to start with to inspire play ideas. Office, waiting room, or dining room chairs can add to the choices and allow chair artists' imaginations to experiment. Padded, vintage, or bent wood chairs instantly change the look of an art room, and the best selection can be made to build a throne or embark on a sleigh to ride. Using chairs in play suggests the flexible use and availability of every item in any art room.

Chair Plays at Home

Studying the way children play with chairs at home offers a range of ideas for art room set-ups. In-home chairs are used as a variety of riding toys. Sturdy chairs are step stools that elevate children. In imaginative creations, chairs are stacked as play blocks to be a lighthouse or an airport control tower. Chairs can be lined up, tipped, or built with to stage performances. Found objects, pillows, toys, or play figures provide accessories for the chair play. Here are some example scenarios of chair play.

> **The drive-through**: There is no honking, but there are many cars pulling up to a drive-through window. Drivers have large orders, and play foods made from found objects are handed to the driver of each chair.
>
> **The auto shop**: Inside a customizing shop, a new installation is in progress. A transformed cup holder is accessorized with a shiny pot cover steering wheel attached with silver duct tape as a dashboard on the back of a chair.
>
> **The racecar**: Two cushiony chairs are on the floor, locked back to back. They are converted into a racecar with the young driver wearing a bike helmet.

Chairs in School

Preparation for play in the art classroom can mean simply moving chairs away from tables, so that students can use them in whatever way they see fit. Chairs can be visibly freed from tables to be borrowed and reconfigured in playing. Letting go of controlling the classroom furniture involves promoting flexibility through stories and playful demonstrations.

Before each class, the art teacher has an opportunity to play the role of mover and re-decorator. It sounds like work, but it's creative fun. Chairs can be shuffled to fashion a scene or suggest a story that invites play ideas. Here are some examples of ways to integrate chairs into art play.

> Position a single chair to act as a shopping cart, a carriage, or a lawn mover—this of course includes providing appropriate sound effects.
>
> Combine chairs to create a park bench, a seesaw, a school bus, or an amusement park ride.
>
> Use magic to turn ordinary chairs into extraordinary space stations, or invent secret words that will turn a stack of chairs into a robot.
>
> Explore possible objects extensions or attachments for the chair. What could be used to turn a chair into an airline seat or a hot air balloon? Wheels made of hoops, a skateboard, or different steering gear can make the chair come alive. Imaginative additions can become skis, wheels, wings, or fuel, all designed for exceptional mobility.
>
> Drape chairs in different fabrics. Dress and accessorize them with umbrellas, or create a surrey with fringe on top. Adding different styles of cushions adds scores of possibilities.
>
> Setting up chairs in different patterns can imply a game, an obstacle course, or act as a shield and space divider. Many chairs can be used to create an indoor sculpture garden or suggest an indoor playground.

Chairs from a secondhand store can act as easels or become a stage, a base set up for activities and displays.

Setting Up a Place That Can Be Altered

The contents of any art room should be set up to be spontaneously changed by the teacher and easily steered into any position by children or students. When they help to move chairs about, they become engaged in a culture of adapting the setting to facilitate an idea. The ability to make changes in the room signals the flexibility allowed for all creative activities. Each shift inspires new play possibilities for what can be placed around a chair, under, or over it. To build a tower, a jail, a stage, or a tower, chairs are one of the most versatile toys in the room.

Depending on the chair arrangement, the art room can feel structured and ordered or be inviting for a fluid and moving adventure through its space. When chairs are not used as a means to restrain students, they can present great opportunities for creating settings that invite playing and contribute to a valuable art experience.

Tables

Children see every space as a playhouse, and home is just a place to colonize, to find nooks and crannies and hidden places to create their own secret playhouses. A closet, under the bed, or even a special drawer can be a place to set up play. Tables in particular are favorite protected domains children use for privacy. Crawling under their table of choice, they can pull the tablecloth low and post a *Do Not Enter* sign to establish that the space is their territory. They can create clubhouses and determine who can be allowed in. Under tables, their work and play can be freer and more fun because they aren't being watched or criticized. It's a space where children can control the light, bring their food and music, and create different play set-ups.

A Place of One's Own

Having a table of one's own with which to play is about having a space to control. Students can take ownership of certain parts of the art room space by crawling under a table and deciding what is to be done inside. An art room can be set up with different tables to offer special nooks, hiding places, private caves to take creative charge. Studios within studios can be created with partitions, covers, domes, or rugs, to separate rooms. Whether or not a child can have his or her own table, having access to tables is important to children to nurture skills as creative builders, decorators, and designers. It is a space of many play possibilities.

The Art of Playing with Tables

Coming into an art room and being invited to climb under the table is a game changer. Setting up for play under desks allows students to move away from the school environment into a fun place that is comfortable and familiar. Students of all ages know that getting under the table is a ticket to different mindsets and creative fantasies.

Moving chairs away from tables shows students they can be objects to use and not just sit at. When desks are freed from rows, they can be playfully regrouped as forts, caves, bridges, tunnels, or mazes. Used individually tables become malls or storefronts or freestanding theaters to showcase performances. Most art room stock can benefit from a variety of tables; folding tables, inflatable tables, or Lego tables offer choices in shapes, surfaces, and scale to inspire play.

Table Transformations

To attract innovative plays, tables have to be imagined as transformable play objects and not class furniture. Part of the transformation of tables involves using creative building materials. Remember, any object—from umbrellas to blankets to toys to boxes—can and should be available to use as additions to a table. To help students find new ways to use tables, teachers can rehearse with them the different ways to angle, group, and realign tables in order to discover their potential for creative uses. The following suggestions offer fresh ways to approach tables as objects for play.

Giftwrapping a table: Giftwrapped as a present with shiny foils, ribbons and bows, a classroom table offers an exciting treat for students and encourages them to imagine their own ways to wrap a table. Papers and fabrics can be stretched around the legs and over the top. They can turn the table into a vintage car that needs a protective car cover, or the table can become a house once they create exterior siding with a long stretch of butcher paper. Stretching plastics around the table legs can create an aquarium. Students can wind and weave ribbons and yarns around the table legs to turn it into a loom.

Fresh grass under the table: Altering the ground under the table changes its potential uses. With a fresh grass carpet beneath a table, it becomes a green house/garden. Or students can spread hay beneath it like a barn. Lining the floor under a table can turn it into a cabana under which to lie. Placing objects like runners, oriental carpet pieces, or a *Welcome* doormat before the table also suggests different play uses.

Rising to new heights: The school table changes when raised over a sturdy platform of blocks, books, or chairs. With the new high ceiling, the table can become a dome or a canopy, or a car wash when hung with fabric strips or ribbons. A table raised over a platform of skateboards can be a bus children take on imaginative field trips without ever having to leave the art room.

Setting the table: Setting up a variety of potential table covers for children to use can encourage creative table play. Drop cloths, formal white tablecloths, vintage pieces of drapery, horse blankets, sheets, quilts, foam, and screening can be tabletops. With stickers, a tabletop becomes a stovetop. Painted table-settings prepare for a smorgasbord of play foods. According to how the table is set, featured items may appear as a store, a flea market, or a restaurant salad bar.

The space between tables: Distances and angles between tables can be varied, set up for plays that emphasize the space in between. These spaces can become canyons for daredevil dolls to jump, and bridges can be designed to help cars cross the dangerous divide. Stretching fabrics over the divide creates a bouncy trampoline with which to test the flight capacity of pencils and other objects.

Turning tables upside down: A table on its side or completely flipped upside down tends to draw immediate attention from students when they enter the art room. The unexpected creates new views that also unlock students' imaginations. Desks can be "jacked up" on any side with a book(s) or turned to expose a new side and ways to play. Table legs can become flagpoles for an upended desk sports arena or, rigged with flashlights and speakers, a stadium for a rock concert.

A continuous path: Tables can be connected to create different shapes and paths. When organized in a line, the space between the tables can become a parade route for toys and other objects. It can become a highway for cars or a runway for planes. Tables can be corralled into a circle racetrack for turtles or Matchbox cars.

Table cities: Tables can be set up as a town or city for an exercise in architectural play. Each table building can wear different façades of curtain, paper, plastic, or mirror walls. Students can use sheets and panels to add to or subdivide buildings.

Table interiors: The table interiors can be model homes where students can create inviting rooms with lavish decors of stuffed pillows and inflatable beach items. Or they can be a cruise ship or a train's first class sleeping car.

Rental properties: Students may be too young to buy a house but not to rent some play space for a class. Add a large *For Lease* sign or a *Will Build to Suit* sign under an art room table space. Students can then take over the "property" with their imaginations to create a high-rise, mall, or a parking garage. The darkened space under a table also makes a great dance club. The dark draping used to cover the underside of the table becomes a canvas to paint for a colorful light show accented by Glow Sticks and toy figures dancing underneath.

Continuing Table Play

Continuing table play children often start at home is useful for students of all ages and at all levels of schooling because it keeps them thinking outside the box, willing to imagine new potential for mundane objects.

Playing Beyond the Art Room

Children's primary art studios are their rooms; however, playing takes place everywhere. Youngsters continually search for special places in which to set up and perform, unusual spaces to conduct creative activities. Instead of trying to contain young artists to one room, nomadic players and explorers need to be accommodated. Certainly it's difficult to have toys and play set-ups all over a home or classroom, but we need to consider that it's important for young artists to gravitate to new places and be inspired by new surroundings.

Art on a school desk is very different than art made under it. Plays that occur in a kitchen are different from those in the laundry room. Art made inside a classroom is different from art inspired by the light and nature in a schoolyard. Moving from classroom surfaces to playing in or around the building encourages students to think in terms of altering spaces and creating installations. The following sections move with children searching for new experiences in different play places, new rooms to design and decorate.

In the Little House

Near my studio in the hills of Woodstock, N.Y., there is a special playhouse we call the "little house." Built in 1936, the small dwelling has been home to many players, including my children and now the grandkids. Outside the box of art rooms and art teachers, the little house offers a direct link to children's art all summer.

When Danielle was six, she was excited to move into the playhouse, filling shopping bags she loaded into a red cart, which included essential supplies and, of course, snacks. Inspired by the birth of her little sister, Danielle used the playhouse each day to stage her stories. During the first day of play, Danielle unveiled her newborn, a doll under her shirt. The baby needed a crib, and she drew the baby's outline on a cardboard box and looked for other building supplies. For pillows and blankets, she collected leaves and wove them together with tape and paint. Stacking old cigar boxes, she assembled a chest of drawers. Fancy wrapping papers cut and shaped into custom diapers completed the infant's ensemble.

Danielle's art was setting up a summer nursery. She illustrated books to show her baby doll and made toys from shiny rocks and special twigs found around the little house. For the doll's birthday party, an entire morning was spent to turn the little house into a party palace. To prevent disturbances, a scarecrow was built to keep angry birds from diving into the window. Danielle formed a pocketbook from a shopping bag, made a valet ticket and keys because she needed to go shopping for the baby.

Her free flow of inventions didn't wait for an art lesson. Throughout the summer, play continued with few dry spells. What Danielle made were not typical school art projects. Moving into her own house opened up boundless imaginative possibilities for things to make and scenarios to perform. There are many places children can wander into to make it their own playground or little house.

Moving Into the Big House

Children are the foremost "renter" of spaces around their home, to be used for a time and then returned to the "owner." They often usurp home closets to create a reading corner, a cave, or a private art studio. Playing in home closets is a significant play that can take root in art classes. To provide studios within studios, rooms within rooms, is the challenge.

Moving under beds, young developers create enclosed shopping centers or covered parking structures. It is not unusual to see a tent popped up in a child's room, or spaces between furnishings draped and designated as an extra bedroom. Childhood "apartments" allow for playing and making creative decisions over spaces and furnishings.

Hallways also attract young adventure seekers and suggest different ways to move and play. Long and winding spaces, stairs, railings allow for different ways to set up and hang forms and roll out canvases and carpets. Hallways have a flow and direction that alters the familiar staging and sequence of play, events, and supplies. The public space invites parades, pulling and driving sculptural creations, and staging action sequences and events. Stepping just outside the controlled zone of a classroom promotes a more relaxed play state. Hallways are passages that lead to other places, suggestions of adventures and anticipation of experiences yet to be determined.

Children roving around the home designate nooks and crannies as play spaces. The nature and feel of each space suggests a different ship or plane to board. One of the oldest private studios for children is the bathtub. Behind the privacy of drawn curtains, endless stories told with props are revealed. Creations with cups and sponges, artistic pouring and bubble icebergs, or synchronized underwater shows offer a vast variety of play. The feel of the tub can be replicated in art class play pools, with or without water. Playing in large boxes, storage containers, crates, baskets, trunks offer similar opportunities as special playrooms.

Playing on the Go

Children spend a great deal of time in vehicles, like the backseats of family cars or school buses. Children embarking on a long family trip or students off on a school bus outing can prepare for vehicle play by bringing art supplies with them. What students make on a trip can be part of a moving display inside and all around the vehicle. Or, children who don't bring materials can benefit from the impromptu offerings of a car space. These often turn to creative moments for testing what can be done with all the stuff that's found in one's surroundings. The messier the car, the more opportunities it offers for building and construction plays. Amazing things can be made from tissues, candy wraps, broken pencils, trays, and cups that would otherwise be considered trash. The seat provides an open canvas and the co-passengers a captive audience for moving performances. Even the scenes outside the car windows can become part of car play. These are creative plays worthy of support.

The Inspiring Outdoors

At the town park, Danielle goes for the swings and the bright yellow climbing apparatus. But, her most creative time is spent on the ground—in the pile of dirt and stones, which she shapes into mountains and excavates as lakes, paths, and bridges. Danielle spreads a towel to climb into a pretend car. She puts on her hat and drives using a Frisbee steering wheel. She finds caves beneath the playground structures and bare shrubs, hidden enclosures she calls her fort. The green wooden park bench she calls a restaurant. Adults are invited while she takes their orders and serves from a kitchen of floor finds. The town park is her imagination and adventure playground.

Artists are inspired by travels and this is very true of young artists. However, many young artists find little time between school and after-school activities to play outside. An important creative behavior to support is children's desire to go outside, to go places, and move. For active children, being forced to sit at the same school desk offers little change in perspectives, surroundings, or surfaces. Art teaching is keeping young bodies and inventive spirits traveling and experiencing new places. Designing trips around the room, hallway, school, and outdoors offers different lights, air, space, and huge grassy or blacktop canvases. Sidewalks or playgrounds offer lines and forms, seasonal raw materials for players. Going outside allows vast options for finding individual places to play.

Each day, special trips can be planned in the room or outside to make the art experience akin to being a world traveler in search of new experiences. Travel cases or tool belts can be designed and outfitted by students to prepare for the excursion, so they can collect souvenirs to import back to the room. Going out with ideas, coming back with prized objects are part of an art class on the move. Between parents and the art teacher, time needs to be made to liberally play and invent on outdoor turf, vast canvases far beyond what classrooms allow.

New Places and New Inspirations

New places lead to new inspirations. Remaining in the same art room every day encourages students to focus on the art on tables and not on the environment. The art becomes stationary, and artistic impulses are less likely to be heeded outside of the designated space. That is why it is important to step outside the art room to explore art as altering and setting up spaces. At home, children play throughout the house and outside. The art room has to recreate this expanse of opportunities to move from room to room, place to place. Children's art needs to keep moving, challenging students to find interesting places to play and install one's art.

4
MATERIALS FOR PLAY AND CREATIVITY

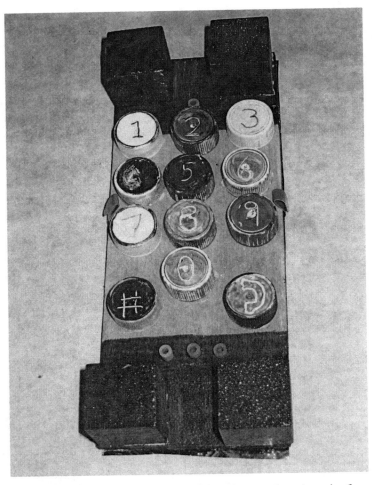

FIGURE 4.0 Play mirrors the present, but offers visionary views into the future.

This chapter looks at the materials that go into the creation of the play-centered art room. The chapter combines overviews of the types of play materials art teachers can integrate into the art class with stories about how children find and use different materials in creative playing and art making. Children amass fortunes in interesting stuff that parents and teachers often consider valueless trash. I provide examples of play props ranging from the conventional to the unexpected as I explore the many resources children discover for found object play. My observations of children's searches for objects and their proposals for inventive uses will ground the reader in developing day-to-day play and art experiences for the 21st-century art room.

Materials for Play and Creativity: Thinking Beyond Traditional Art Supplies

Crayon Lectures

Sponsored by a crayon company, I was invited to give lectures that accompany children's art shows presented at universities. The gigs went well for a while, until a company representative heard my talk. In the presentation, I mentioned that the way children view everything as an art supply reflects both present and future trends in contemporary art. I also mentioned that this company does not have a monopoly and that the environment is the world's largest art supplier. Oops!

After an amicable end to this sponsorship, I continue to urge art teachers not to be intimidated by official art supply lists, stores, catalogues, or crayon companies. Instead, teachers should reaffirm what children instinctively know: that creative play supplies that are not prepackaged are more exciting, especially when they get to find and choose what they want to use for their creative endeavors. Thus, part of art teaching should include deputizing the student to "shop" for art supplies everywhere because the most interesting art supplies have yet to be discovered.

Traditional Art Supplies and Play Art Supplies

In school, students wait to be told what tools they are supposed to use in art, and the emphasis tends to be on traditional art supplies. These supplies include a narrow list of objects such as paintbrushes, clay, paper, and crayons that are generally used for conventional art projects like paintings, sculptures, and drawings. To create students who may one day push the bounds of art means to encourage young artists to pick up, save, and use any material in their creations. New art lies just beyond the discovery of an interesting object to play with.

Children already find and play with a variety of unusual objects. An old bike wheel is turned into a carousel. A bike seat becomes a bull's head. Play blocks are for building, but why not books, or pillows? A brush is for painting, but why not paint with plastic fishing worms, rocks, or combs? Puppets are amazing, but why not put on a show with gardening tools? Everything from pretzels and buttons to dolls and old pipes is an art supply to a child. These play art supplies can be used to make traditional art projects like paintings and sculptures, but they can also be used for performances, displays, and new art forms that have yet to be imagined.

Getting beyond what we can already visualize is the point of using play art supplies, which can include any object that someone decides to play with. A newspaper can be read but also explored as a canvas. Hot Wheels can be combined with other objects for a sculpture or, with a little paint on the wheels, become a new kind of paintbrush. Even traditional art supplies can become play supplies when used in unexpected ways. A paintbrush can be tried as a stick horse or perform as a broom. Crayons can be melted down and used to create new colors or even be used for sculpture. A canvas can become an apron, a tablecloth, or a tent. Maintaining a willingness to play with everything, to call anything an art supply, can be an important result of taking an art class. That's why art classes should continue to build on what children already do best: letting their imagination run free.

Open Minds Encourage Art

This chapter is more than just about materials. It's about conveying a sense of openness as to what art is and what art can be. To teach art in a contemporary world, we have to be able to invent the tools, develop the techniques, and find materials by exploring all places and all sources.

The whole point of play in art, as I have discussed, is that play can teach old tools new tricks to encourage fresh and innovative art, and it can use new tools for both innovative and conventional art. The way to facilitate inspiration in the art classroom is to get beyond prescriptive thinking about art supplies; to encourage the play that keeps the notion of art open; to be willing to look at all tools and media as possibilities. That is why, throughout this chapter, I will provide examples and recommendations meant to encourage new approaches to art education that encourage artistic exploration by rethinking materials for play and creativity.

The Self-Serve Art Room

A full-service gas station used to mean that an attendant did the work: pumped the gas, checked the oil, and cleaned the windshield. Now, most gas stations are self-service: you take care of your car, and the station serves the driver's shopping needs, like a roadside shopping mall. Children's approach to play and art at home reflects this self-service kind of atmosphere, where they take care of their creative

FIGURE 4.1 Players showcase their art inside containers such as shopping bags.

needs while shopping around their room, their home, and their environment to find supplies of all kinds. However, many art rooms still follow the full-service model, where the art teacher does the work by providing ideas and setting up the supplies necessary to make it work.

One of the reasons a play-based approach to teaching art is so effective at inspiring the imagination and developing young artists is because it provides guidance and tools that designate the art classroom a self-service space. This kind of open space demands exploration and experimentation. It encourages self-reliance and hands-on searching. It puts the children, and their dreams, in charge of the artistic process and thus encourages habits for life-long artistic production and vision.

Self-Service Turns Students into Artists

In traditional art classrooms, the teacher's plan generally prescribes what materials are to be used in each art lesson. However, outside the classroom, artists must decide upon their own materials. The artistic process generally does not take dictation. In other words, making art means making decisions. Choosing what can be done with a material or how a found object can be used is fundamental to the artistic process, so an art class that teaches the student-artist to make decisions provides a more realistic art experience.

In art classes that emphasize divergent thinking and creative behavior, students should be encouraged to see and enumerate the multitude of possibilities in objects and in their environment. Art room exercises can include having students brainstorm as many uses as they can for any find. They can include allowing children to draft any object into their play in unusual ways, such as using a paint roller as farm equipment. Exercises can also include a time for show and tell where students exhibit their finds.

Self-Service Demands Freedom of Use

A self-service art room must necessarily be an open room, meaning students must have free access to drawers, closets, containers, and secret compartments. The fewer things locked away or off-limits, the more students are reminded that the art room is theirs. Anything can be borrowed and added to play and an artwork. I often jest by saying, "If I am not wearing it you can use it!" Through unofficial signs, remarks and gestures, an art room can be physically unlocked, open, and inviting to players. The idea is for students to have as much access as possible to the room's content.

Of course, as a public space, an art room has to have some closets and drawers that are off-limits. To prevent all the paints from being used by the end of the first school week, it's important to separate them. If the art class does not have a separate supply storeroom, there needs to be one carved out from the art room space, differentiating art supply storage from shopping sites for found objects intended for shoppers. The key to creating freedom is to maintain a sensible balance of order and access.

Self-Service Requires Patience

Many parents and teachers tend to see children as hoarders of useless stuff, of junk. Unable to imagine what purpose a broken vacuum, random doll parts, or the plastic toys from kid's meals might serve in the creative process, they are more likely to throw such items out or disallow them in the classroom. However, teaching art with an open mind to student-directed innovation means being tolerant about junk, messes, and process. It means stepping back and listening to student-artist needs. It means taking students seriously and inquiring about their finds and the many plans for using them.

To encourage creativity, parents and art teachers should allow for abundant opportunities for students of all ages to freely search and add to their material collections. They also need to be patient with children who might initially struggle to free their imaginations or who take a lot of time to search and find. After all, being encouraged to make choices on their own might be a new experience for children, especially as students who are not used to such freedom.

Ultimately, a play-based, self-service art room takes student fun seriously and does not discriminate or assign preference to forms, tools, and objects. Children as artists find beauty and use in the useless, and they can teach adults much about the creative process. In order to do so, they must be accepted and respected as the inventors they already are.

Self-Service Allows for the Discovery of Art

Using only standard or traditional art supplies and assignments sends the message that all art is known and all the same. Using non-traditional materials and assigning more play-based, imaginative assignments shows them that art is discovery, that there is art that has yet to be found. Artists need a broad license. If art classes are to sow the seeds for new art, they must have access to open, creative fields suggesting that art is all around them.

Shopping Sites in the Classroom

Learning to "shop," to select objects and tools for play and art materials, is a key to self-service art, and it often begins at home. Children like to take every opportunity to collect treasures outside of the home in their day-to-day experiences. In an active child's playroom, there is usually tons of good stuff around to select from. Parents who are interested in preserving their child's playing cannot rush to clean out everything or criticize collectors for saving and storing unusual finds. To ensure that children have the opportunity to collect and be surrounded by inspiring objects is a parental responsibility.

A teacher has the same responsibility, and an art room can provide that same kind of excitement of the playroom when it's filled with things that students want to save and collect. Think of the art room as one large treasure chest that offers endless stimulating opportunities to search. The treasures provided can help students of all ages find ways to be engaged at school and experience the

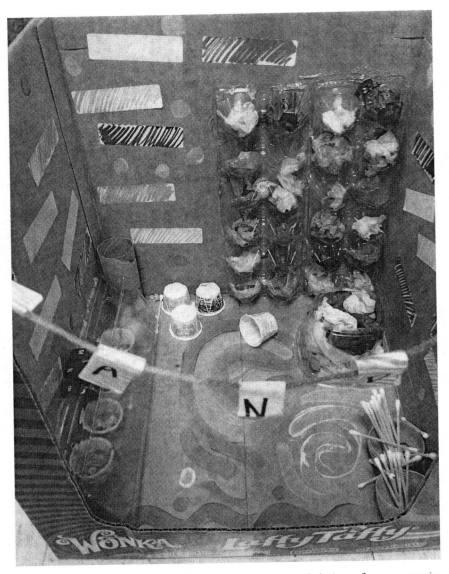

FIGURE 4.2 Incubating inside boxes, the new in art and design often appears in children's playhouses.

fun of being empowered as players. Students love coming to a room set up for shopping pleasures not only to play and make art but also to be with others who are excited about interesting forms and collecting.

Recognizing students as treasure seekers and motivated collectors of the unusual helps instructors plan their art classes. Searching and uncovering, digging, and opening containers to find surprises can be encouraged through the way the art room is designed. An art room set up to stimulate shopping teaches students to find what's interesting, to recognize that their environment can be the largest of all art supply stores, and to help them understand that art can be found anywhere.

From Home Shopping to School Shopping

Before I drop the children off, I read them the usual riot act, reminding them to deposit their play contraband on the backseat. These items are generally not welcome in school and are often confiscated by teachers. The children thus dutifully empty their pockets and other hiding places, knowing their little toys and assorted objects will lay dormant until I return to pick the children up, and they can return to play.

If children have the opportunity to play in their art class, then these objects—and the imagination they engage—don't have to lay dormant on backseats, at home, or (let's face it) in the other more clever hiding places children find to illegally import their play goods. Think of the items students bring from home as prefabricated play materials that the children have already tested, played with, and loaded with ideas. These items contribute immensely to the stock of art room shopping.

Donations for shared public use are fun to bring to class when they can be shared with others. In small plastic baggies marked "For Art Class Use," one student unveils a selection of bottle caps she divided by colors. Another treasure collector carries a cigar box containing an assortment of candy wrappers. Setting up an art room for play takes many willing and interested contributors who can be deputized to constantly search and save stuff. Excitement and satisfaction and loads of ideas come with the bearers of such gifts.

Letting students bring their items from home not only takes some of the onus of populating the art room with play supplies off the instructor, but it also encourages the same sense of freedom of discovery that children experience in the many other shopping sites they encounter outside of school.

Designing the Room for Shopping

Serious adult flea market shoppers arrive early, in order to be the first to go through everything. They don't go to the flea market for what they need but for the adventure of freely inspecting, discovering objects, and imagining what they could be used for. Ideas emerge from just being around interesting things set out on tables or on the grass. Planning for an art room shopping site is like setting up a great flea market that students cannot wait to enter and investigate.

Art teachers can think of themselves as flea market owners creating inviting shopping displays or aisles. Each school day is a grand opening for play and art for which art teachers can prepare by having fun stuff on hand to entice and surprise playful treasure seekers. Before students enter the class, the teacher can spread unusual objects throughout the room to encourage creative selection, or "shopping." After all of the shopping sites have been stocked by the instructor and the students, students can collect their goods with shopping bags they've created and stamped "Top Secret." Or different bags, boxes, carrying cases can be rented daily to contain students' shopping selections. Art room trays, baskets, and play-shopping carts are ready to be loaded. It's all about finding interesting treasures and creating inviting shopping sites that encourage self-service and selection. And students are always ripe and ready to use the found items to make things. That is what real play and art incentives require.

Filling Shopping Containers

Even the containers students use for their shopping can be interesting, can make a room inviting and always surprising. Containers with many drawers, such as tackle boxes or make-up containers, are fun to sort through. Backpacks and sand buckets, when filled with toy parts, discarded hardware, and packaging materials, invite curiosity. Interesting bins, vintage trashcans, and old toy chests turn an ordinary room into a special market. All containers should be filled and refilled with fun stuff to make the art room a favorite store and place to shop.

Picturing an Art Room Flea Market

Here are some examples of the ways a creativity-inspiring, play-based classroom might set up shop to encourage treasure hunting.

> An old scout trunk is on the floor under the window filled with such interesting forms as hair curlers, switches, knobs, and bike parts. Help yourself! Nearby on a folding hotel luggage stand, a suitcase is jam-packed with unusual fabric samples, colored extension cords, plastic jar lids of different colors in plastic bags along with buttons, slightly rusted washers, and canning seals.
>
> Springs, plugs, old keys, buttons, toy prizes, puzzle parts are displayed in an old sewing box that has many compartments. Lampshades and beach balls are exhibited in a child's play pool. Inside a worn tire are parts of hoses and pipes to look through.
>
> In the back of the room is a library card catalogue cabinet. The many drawers with shiny brass pulls are labeled: Rare Stickers, Countertop Samples, Designer Band-Aids, Rocks and Shells, Ribbons, Plastic Lures, Doll Parts, and Puzzle Parts.
>
> Under the file cabinet is a scuffed old black hatbox. Upon inspection there are layers of trading cards, dominoes, coasters, candy wrappers, slide mounts, floral tapes, and Post-it pads on the bottom.

In the corner of the room is an old train-shaped toy box. Open the freight door to find assorted restaurant trays, foil pans, exposed x-rays, PVC pipes, foam packing shapes, and segments of striped garden hoses.

On the side wall of the room is an old newspaper stand. Old thrift store baskets are on each level, along with a display of toy parts, game controllers, wheels, assorted sponges, weathered gardening gloves, cork mats, and rubber sink liners.

Under tables are different color laundry baskets, each with a different collection, such as carpet samples, tiles, flip flops, different cup holders, aged phones, and small gold picture frames.

Outdoor trashcans are not used for trash. Their sculptural-presence lines a side of the room as a store display of larger items, such as assorted wood and sidewalk pieces, used bike seats, thrift store belts, straw baskets and hats, and a myriad of thought-provoking plastic and cardboard parts and containers.

In the ever-revolving inventory of an art room flea market, items may be here today and gone tomorrow, but there will be other finds. Shopping through containers can be as much fun as looking for things to refresh their contents, a task contributed to by teachers, parents, and young explorers. Will it be alarm clocks, or an assortment of used brushes? No one knows what will be imported for shoppers tomorrow.

Creative Shop-a-holics

To instill the values of artistic shopping, the art room set-up can be an important demonstration. An art room that inspires players to act in creative ways is a discovery place, a place to constantly discover new things. It is a room designed for choices about where to work, what to do, what can be used. Neither art teachers nor monitors can predict every student-artist's needs. That is why play supplies should include all kinds of interesting found objects and not just art supplies. The contents of the room can be renewed and changed constantly. Everything belongs to everyone, and everyone is a shopper and contributor to supplies.

Shopping Sites: The Way Children Search for Materials

There is nothing like the feeling of discoveries made on one's own. The freedom to shop any and everywhere provides the pleasures of discovery, the thrill of the hunt. To be permitted to shop all over, to look at everything as possibilities, to feel independent in searching and deciding what one wants to touch, manipulate, and transform is essential in playing and art making. In the previous section, I explained the importance of shopping in the classroom as part of the play-based art process. In this section, I provide some examples of

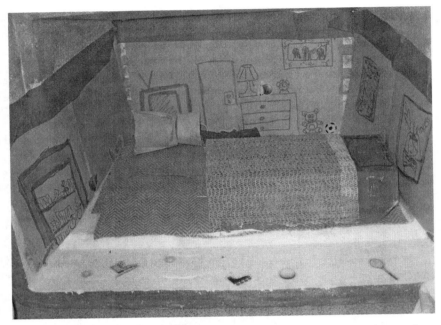

FIGURE 4.3 Children constantly plan and redesign their rooms. An art class needs to have a similar freedom in leasing.

specific shopping sites outside the classroom that teachers can replicate inside the classroom.

Home Shopping Network

After evoking guilt through the customary complaint that "you never play with me," I sit on the floor of Emilie's studio-room, waiting for her to look around the house for stuff. Play often requires her to first look around the house and shop for supplies. Emilie scavenges the medicine cabinet to find interesting tapes and cotton balls. She moves into the kitchen to stock up on lids in the refrigerator and plastic containers from the trash. Borrowing a few coffee filters and cupcake tins, she moves on to look inside my toolbox for loose parts. I wait with patience knowing that the gathering of supplies is not only pleasurable for her, but an important means of finding ideas.

Children can collect things dropped on the floor, reach into containers and shelves, and pursue treasure hunting under kitchen counter cabinets. They can scavenge through pocketbooks, checking inside for anything interesting. Home explorers look in closets and drawers, and seldom a package enters a house without it being checked by volunteer-inspectors. Cupboards, boxes, and cubbies in the classroom can be populated with the same kind of regular household items to provide places to search.

Shopping Outside the House

Each spring, the rain dismantles our driveway. For the adults, this season means work: moving the many stones and rocks back in place to make the road usable. For Emilie, this season means driveway shopping: joyfully gathering materials for her imaginative plans. Like an old prospector, she sifts through the site for "rock candy" in the most interesting forms and colors.

Digging and excavating are a timeless means of treasure hunting for tons of materials brought to the art class. Instructors can transport a load of river rocks with an assortment of gardening stones in a red wheelbarrow to the back of the school for a dig site. Play pools of sand or rocks can be used in the classroom for art class archeologists, paleontologists, and other creative seekers.

Supermarket Shopping

At the supermarket, Mom gets one cart for the groceries, and Emilie gets one cart to hold the "free stuff" that she calls "art supplies" that she finds around the store. A curious clerk might ask, "What are you going to do with this?" Used to explaining her finds with great insight to anyone interested in her art, Emilie might elaborate about renovating the playhouse, providing details about the intended use for each unusual box, padding material, produce tie, or advertising label. Emilie also finds things to add to the play grocery store she is building.

But the creative fun doesn't stop once she's selected her own goods. It continues as Emilie continues to shop in the car amongst the goods her mother purchased. Carefully opening a cell phone just purchased, she sets aside the foam forms and cardboard dividers. The bright red netted sack that used to contain onions is also claimed, separated from its contents, joining her supply pile on the seat. None of these items go to waste in an imaginative child's play, which is something teachers can consider as they gather their own supplies.

Park Shopping

On a family walk, participants often have conflicting goals. Adults see the walk as exercise and an important remedy for a sedentary lifestyle. Kids tend to slow things down because they see it as an opportunity to browse nature. They check out the scenery, investigate things on the ground, pick up and pocket new finds, and generally turn a walk through the park into a fruitful shopping trip. School-yard shoppers can enjoy the same experiences. Few brushes or actual art supplies are needed to paint or play outdoors when nature provides.

Construction Shopping

Few things are more fun than building supplies. A trip to Lowe's or Home Depot, or a child's home undergoing renovation, yields daily treasures: samples, counter tops, and floor pieces populate building material heaven. Should the school ever undergo remodeling, think of it as an opportunity to offer children new shopping sites. Just watching the daily trucks unloading can offer amazing inspiration, but renovation also offers a constant flow of mounds, mountains, and skyscraper-size stacks of fresh supplies to explore.

Garbage Shopping

Trash days offer a street paved with prospects, and taking out the trash doesn't have to be a chore for children who get to excavate from the can. While this might not sound appealing to parents, they should be respectful of children's prospecting efforts and offer guidance and support. Parents can even join children on a walk around the block to explore other curbs and cans or offer the pull cart to use for the freelance collector. The art class can encourage favorite curbside secrets to be shared. Maybe someone knows that Monday is a good day to hit the bike store dumpsters, when choice bike parts are available. Maybe a student has an adventure to share about following the clean up crew at the local movie theater and amassing fantastic items for candy wrap and ticket stub collections. The art class can also offer up its own waste cans, maybe even wrapped in signs that say *Welcome to Browsers.*

Takeout Shoppers

The importance of takeout varies between parents and youngsters. Adults seek quick meals, while children seek either a kid's meal toy or interesting materials: utensils, burger wraps, coffee cup rings, drink caddies, and many other supplies. In the art class, there can be lively trades of unusual lids and fries boxes to add to individual collections.

Yard Sale Shopping

While ladies shop for clothes and bargain jewelry, the shine that draws many kids is the chrome of yesterday's technology. Children can find old computers, video games, hair dryers, clocks, and other home appliances to be disassembled or unscrewed as they plan as future engineers–artists–serious tinkerers. Items selected for parts are available for practically nothing for those willing to haul them away. A good art school or MIT education can start with good garage sales or a free pass to Goodwill stores. So, art classes do well to provide the pliers and screwdrivers, duct tape and glue guns, with which students can remodel, repurpose, or repair their yard sale finds.

Support for the Search

Parents and art teachers need to support the creative search and collecting of the exciting and free by commending and not reprimanding children's choices in open and visionary supply finds. Parents and teachers can reinforce each other by being proud of the treasures students find, by taking the initiative to go into the trash, or by confidently asking the manager in a store for things a child may want to use to play and create with. These reinforcements help us prepare for an art world where there are no limitations.

A frequent home and art class conversation can be asking children's opinions about and clues for places to find supplies. Just ask students for the best source for wood and sit back to take notes. The family shed, the school's theater department, the frame store all throw out great stuff. The Habitat for Humanity store is filled with unusual railing, fence parts, kitchen cabinet doors, and other great finds. What about the great yard sticks and paint stirrers free for the asking? The children's answers will give insight into the mindset that can invent the future of art.

Toy Materials

Toys provide ready-made play materials. They may seem rather conventional, but toys have a special appeal for students, many of whom probably either have favorite toys at home or happy memories of their favorite toys when they were

FIGURE 4.4 Play performances are a prelude for art in all media.

younger. That is why including toys in an art class changes a child's attitude towards art and what can be done in an art class. When children's favorite things, toys, fill the art class, they are in touch with home and community, with their past, with the real things that inspire artists as players.

Toys are creative materials for play in the art room in that they promote creative building, designing, and performances. Art teaching cannot ignore toys as art supplies and still hope to invoke the play spirit in students. A respect for students as players needs to include an understanding of the importance of toys in furthering the act of playing. It also requires parents and teachers to create environments in which toys are welcome, to set up art rooms with objects of interest to motivate playing. An art room that welcomes toys as something important supports and values children's feelings and interests.

Basic Toys to Collect

Not every toy is helpful or appropriate for school. Selecting that special toy to be housed in an art class is an important decision. Multi-purpose toys invite a wide range of playing and creative actions. Toys without instructions or rules let children be in control with their imagination. Toys that can be extended or built upon, that require children to build or imagine settings and landscapes can constantly be refreshed in creative use. Art room toys need to be infinitely playable, simply reshaped by play acts and new ideas.

Art classes for all levels and ages need a substantial collection of old and new block sets. Garage sales and secondhand stores are good sources for gathering large quantities of classic building toys that promote plays for all ages. And an old freight train shaped toy box on wheels is an example of a dual-purpose container/toy for housing the blocks. The train can churn a block mix, instead of holding expensive, neatly packaged sets. Old Jenga pieces, Eames blocks, Tinker Toys, Legos, puzzle pieces, and alphabet blocks can be mixed with newer Playskool classics, Dominos, and Tub Block foam pieces in bold colors. Shoppers do the sorting and selecting and then decide on usage.

A rolling Plexiglas aquarium makes another good showcase for figurines. There can never be enough small play pals, Polly Pockets, or action figures to pose, animate, or create environments for. The more dolls, fast-food toy prizes, bobble heads, and toy horses children have at their disposal, the more ideas and scenarios they can explore in their play.

Old lunchboxes with locks can secure fierce dinosaurs, to be cautiously opened and let out one by one. Interesting containers and ways of packaging classroom toys not only make their appearance in class functional, but the nature, signage, illustrated stickers, and security covers add to the surprise and fun of the opening act.

Toys with wheels can turn seated students into active players. At most yard sales, one can find old skateboards, roller skates, toy shopping carts, old bikes, and just tires and furniture wheels to place in a classroom display. A corner shelf can house stacks of Hot Wheels cars collected individually and stored in toy carry cases. The cars can be selected for testing bridges and roads, racetracks and drive-in worlds created by students. Students find many uses for putting their ideas on wheels to ride on, to pull, or to push.

Don't forget that students can contribute to the selection of play supplies in the classroom, and letting them bring toys and other items from home only increases the class inventory. The stuffed animals, dolls, and other favorite toys that students bring are always more fun to dress, cast in plays, have model for paintings, and ask to participate in fashion shows, than the other anonymous creatures who may live in the classroom.

The lists of toys that can be part of an art class play supply stock are endless. And there's no such thing as an official toy. If a student wants to imagine a little rock band using actual rocks, then that rock is an appropriate toy. It's doing the work of sparking the imagination and encouraging the child to dream.

Recycling Toys and Toy Parts

Toys also don't have to be spotless or even in one piece to be used in play. A painted fruit crate of over 100 Barbie arms and legs can be set up for art class shoppers to add to any figurative inventions. This same box can include other doll parts, doll shoes, action figure helmets, sunglasses, and other miscellaneous accessories. Depositing toy truck tires or random doll eyes in the treasury of toy parts can lead to a wealth of play ideas.

Old Atari game controllers, broken bikes, toy guitars that no longer work can still find a home in the art classroom. Out of commission toys still supply incentives and suggest ideas to be completed by customizations and imaginary plays. Children are prolific inventors and can work with anything from toys and toy parts to everyday materials such as straws, napkins, pencils, or Q-tips. Well-stocked toy part boxes support figurative innovation and help in detailing.

Art Room Toy Factory

An art class can be not only a place to bring and play with toys, but also a toy factory, where children make toys called art to play with. There is great joy and motivation in an art class that promotes making things to take home to display or to play with. An art room that's also a toyshop provides wood and fabric, paper and glue, and many other materials to build dolls, playgrounds and shelters for other toys, whatever their imagination instigates. In other words, toys lead the play and the content of the art made in class.

Keeping Toys for Art

Each toy has a story, suggests an adventure or fantasy. Toys are special vehicles for the imagination. The argument is to let students of all ages keep their toys. Instead of selling them at yard sales or donating them, let students of all ages bring their stuffed animals or "significant others" to art class. They already sneak them into school, carry them in pockets and lunchbox safes, and attach them to backpacks. Toys are not a distraction in the art classroom, they are an inspiration!

Art Tool Materials

Young children investigate and use drawing tools and brushes as playfully and freely as other toys. My son Jacob (at age 7) asked to borrow a screwdriver. He used the screwdriver to methodically dissect a drawing pencil. From the way he handled the instrument, I was sure he was to become a surgeon. Interested in what was rolled up inside, Jacob carefully removed each section of black lead with the scalpel. Freeing the lead from its casing allowed for an amazing freedom in drawing. Jacob rolled the lead over paper towels and scratched into a cutting board found in the kitchen.

FIGURE 4.5 A screwdriver is a scalpel to unlock and take apart a world contained inside, so it can be discovered and restructured.

I imagined this to be an isolated incident, until I observed my youngest daughter collecting broken pencil points. In old black Kodak film canisters, Ana saved broken lead as a miniature drawing kit. She selected individual points to create fine line drawings, and she grouped "bouquets" of pencil points by planting them in new handles of foam and clay for more creative lines. Playing with tools as experimental materials in these exemplary ways provides new techniques to mark surfaces, invent, draw, and paint.

As these examples show, children approach learning generally as experimental play. When they enter school, they find education not to be based on their experiences and inventions. Instead, students are told how things work and how everything is to be done. There is a correct way to sharpen a pencil or hold a brush. These are obstacles to playful experimenting in a world in which the correct way and a single path to learning is practiced and rewarded. How to make art, what to do with tools, is not presented as playful discovery. There are rules and expectations, techniques and principles that are clearly demonstrated. What other conclusion can young artists come to but that there is one way to do art: the correct way. Under such conventional adult art rules, there is no need to play to discover unique ways of doing things, for such innovation as taking a pencil apart.

Deconstructed Baseball Caps

Observing a middle school lesson recently, I noticed the importance of students playing with tools and materials before they are asked to make art with them. The teacher I observed gave students an interesting visual history of baseball caps as an introduction and ended with a challenge for new designs. Students can sometimes be reluctant to make significant alterations to an object. They may be afraid to damage the item or have difficulty picturing possible changes. Or students may be so used to being shown how and what to do in other classes that they can't just start to play with the caps in a creative way.

The art teacher had a good idea to address such reluctance. He brought out some sacrificial hats and started a game of cutting and disassembling them, removing first part of the visor. He loosened the red lining and used it to wrap the sides in bright fabric. "Fabric is to play with," the teacher repeated the mantra and students joined in finding creative paths to restructuring the form and surface of caps. With everyone deeply involved in fabric play, it was no longer a hat but an open form from which they could spin off countless new forms and ideas. A baseball cap, a canvas, or any other form needs to be freely played with—punctured, twisted, creased, and dismantled—to be experienced freshly and to inspire original possibilities. Even a sheet of paper placed before students has to be explored and played with in order for students to look at it freshly and find new ways to address the shape and surface.

Play that involves dismantling tools and materials and putting them together, like cutting apart a hat and reconstructing a hat out of unrelated objects, presents important practice opportunities for innovators. Sorting through serving trays, dust pans, lamp shades, and woven baskets to make a cap provides opportunities to see a baseball cap not as a static form and idea but a dynamic one to be explored without reservation. As I've established, every art tool or supply, technique or truth in art can be investigated by playing. Drawing, painting, sculpture, and baseball hats need to be presented as items to be freshly discovered by each student. Even old tools can be taught new tricks and conventional supplies can be playfully handled.

Art teaching is encouraging individuals to find out what drawing is and could be. It is a preparation for the long journey of inventing painting and discovering art. Therefore, art classes need to be occupied with providing opportunities for fresh starts and not with dispensing old and used formulas. Starting fresh may include such play as the following examples.

Play with art tools by hiding them and asking for substitutes. Starting a painting lesson and forgetting to bring the paintbrush . . . does the lesson fail, or succeed when new brushes are found and invented outdoors or in the art class? Finding substitutes for any traditional art tool and material opens a path to the new. Draw with grass dipped into ink, or paint with funnels to discover new ways of drawing and painting. No paper for a drawing lesson? Borrowing hallway posters, searching through the trash or the newspapers and floor tiles the custodian left in the art room suggests new drawing surfaces and ideas.

Play with art tools by pretending to be a first time user. Practice new ways of setting art in motion. Pretend to be a first time user of a pencil, or any traditional tool, to investigate new grips and pressures, ways to adjust and explore the possibilities of the tool.

Play with art tools by adding new handles or extensions. Release tools from routine approaches by taping a drawing tool at the end of a fishing rod, for example. This allows for remote controlling at a distance, with different sways and bounces of the point. Paintbrushes can be clamped to antennas or rakes. A marker taped to a screwdriver, a brush to a fly swatter, a crayon to feather duster promotes different ways of drawing and painting.

Play with art by building a collection of non-art tools. Using a hairbrush, toothbrush, or shaving brush makes painting humorous and playful. A collection of old vacuum cleaner attachments provides for new painting acts. Barbeque tongs, make-up brushes, and housecleaning brushes of all kinds ensure playful new painting adventures.

Alter traditional art tools with grooming. Style a paintbrush before using it. Curl, braid, wrap, or shorten bristles, add fabrics, and prepare the brush for painting and playing.

Breaking Tool Rules

The theme of searching for how to draw, or paint, leads to memorable play acts and unique media discoveries. Instead of art demonstrations for everyone to learn the same watercolor technique, art classes can be set up for students to play with water and colors. Any kitchen drawer brought to school reinvents the theme of painting. With the availability of basters, spatulas, funnels, and eyedroppers, students play with Kool-Aid and other food colors over kitchen surfaces such as napkins and paper towels. Outdoors, watercolor techniques are restored with water guns and plastic watering cans moving colors over outdoor surfaces. In the winter different painting techniques are explored over the white blankets of snow. Every art tool can be tried as a toy and each media can be invented and given new rules, discovered by each player. These creative acts thus empower students to broaden the realm of their imagination at all stages of the art process.

Tech Materials

My granddaughter Emilie lives with our iPhone, plays with our iPods, and uses our Mac computer. Yet, one can also regularly find Emilie happily creating in my studio. In school, Emilie's fourth-grade elementary room has computer stations

FIGURE 4.6 Anything turned upside down and played with suggests a new life, such as the trashcan that evokes a new home design.

and five iPads, but in art class there are easels and time to draw and paint. Emilie is growing up drawing on the computer, using Photo Booth to make humorous pictures, and painting on retired kitchen cabinet doors. Her dual art worlds describe the story of today's art classes in which technology shares a room with the handmade.

Children are used to participating in both worlds, yet, some art teachers feel tension between technology and the art they were taught to make and teach. There are art teachers who ignore technology and say that students have enough screen time, so their art class offers an important humanizing balance. Conversely, many younger art teachers who were raised with video games and remote controllers are happy to offer the upper hand to technology, and not bother with the "messy" arts.

The results of the duel in contemporary art classes have yet to be determined, but there is no doubt that many of today's young students coming to art are experienced and comfortable playing with technology. Thus, a playful and exploratory approach to gadgets and art materials can be important to encourage at home and in school. Playing with technology also offers new ways to think about traditional media, to find new art moves, and possibilities for cross-fertilization. Here are some examples of the creative ways technology can be used.

Technology as Magic

Ever wonder why children love to push elevator buttons? They do it because it seems fun but also because they constantly seek to experiment with technology, to better understand what it can do. Children know that remotes have mighty powers that are controlled by the taps of their fingertips. They like to press the garage opener and marvel at the capacity within the small clicker to raise a giant door. Emilie believes in clicker magic and talks about inventing one for trees, so she can grow them at will and rearrange our backyard landscape. In her imaginative hands, remote controllers are magic wands to direct objects, move images, or even control the stars and universe.

Remote-Clicking the Imagination

Children who log countless hours in video gaming can take their technological interest into the art room to build pretend remote controllers and dreams for their use. Brought from home, a fluffy, plumed feather duster can be transformed by adding instructions for on/off, speed/rotations, and lift/drop. A carrot can be wrapped in foil and inscribed as a remote control stick. These new remotes can be used to create experimental performances. Covering and wrapping up objects and labeling instructions for their uses create new clicker ideas.

Thanks to a collection of space age game controllers from Goodwill, students can imagine many new ways to play with their world. As an art tool for the imagination, one student pretends controlling stuffed animals, and another narrates and illustrates the magic carpet ride they take. A remote controller wired to a spoon is a joystick for an unusual meal. A sponge is taught to paint and a robot takes drawing lessons on a paper screen. Imaginary remote control play leads students to ideas of playfully controlling their breakfast cereal, toy dinosaurs, and art tools. Dustpans, a fly swatter, a scissor, a hairbrush are all granted super powers in play that attaches them to clickers. In a world of remote controlled lights, printers, milking cows, and fighting wars, an art class lab offers a glimpse into a future where technology and art work in concert, thanks to the inventive play of students.

Creative Players in a Tech-Based World

When we adults need help with our smart phones, we don't always go to the Apple Genius Bar because we often have little tech geniuses living right in our house. Even our youngest grandchildren play with the iPhone and know many of its functions. In the art class, students can extend their knowledge and interests in technology as material for play by drawing and building new ideas for smarter phones and other technological devices we have yet to imagine. This is how art technology can become art.

There's no question that technology is a major agent of change in the 21st century, and it certainly seems that children pretend and play imaginatively less the more their imaginative drive and actions go online. This reality is a concern every art teacher has to consider. However, technology's presence doesn't have to preclude play. Children can use it imaginatively, playfully, and in pretend ways. For example, after receiving her dream present—an American Girl Doll—my Emilie makes a pretend phone for the doll, so she can text her. Technology and pretend here go hand in hand. When approached thoughtfully and with a commitment to play, the art class and home studio can productively involve technology. After all, it's new ideas that matter, and children have them in abundance. Play is the most important work of children and the key ingredient in discovery and display of creative ideas—no matter how that play comes about. Play is children's way of brainstorming, problem-solving, seeing new possibilities, and inventing the future. Technology may seem destined to turn active minds into passive ones, but when children learn to play with technology imaginatively, they create a new destiny for themselves.

Packaging Materials

Recently, three colossal boxes arrived at our door containing a stainless steel kitchen table we had ordered. The truck driver complained about the weight he had to schlep, while my granddaughter Emilie kept her eyes on the prizes coming her way. While the table held little interest for her, she could not wait to dig inside the enormous boxes. After the overly burdened delivery person deposited the boxes near the kitchen, Emilie eagerly helped open the taped sides and began removing layers of protective packaging, until she triumphantly presided over a mountain of great wrapping materials.

Having gained access to a rare and unexpected art supply haul, Emilie was ready to play and prepared her plans to build mansions for her favorite American Girl dolls. She stacked white foam shapes, gathered the smartly crafted corner protectors, and carefully folded the several different kinds of plastic wraps. Emilie even noticed the exotic beauty of the tying materials and saved the unusual tools and screw packets for her art studio (her room). For weeks, the giant boxes and packing materials provided motivation to make art after school. One day, she painted and stickered bunk bed constructions. Another day, she designed ultramodern foam chairs and carved foam picture frames for her room. What started as a simple ringing of the doorbell became one of Emilie's most memorable unpacking adventures and greatest art find.

As Emilie's design and construction progressed, her artistic output became a regular part of my own art class daily show and tell. The students followed with great interest each of Emilie's new play creations and had many ideas to add. This is one example of how unconventional play materials can inspire as well as teach us about the possibilities of art. So, while toys and technology have much to offer, it's important to include other types of materials in a play-based art classroom.

School Deliveries

Schools offer a number of exciting delivery occasions for students. Not only deliveries for the cafeteria but also deliveries for supplies and books happen regularly. In a school where students are encouraged to focus on hallway discards, students receive a valuable license to collect materials and ideas as important preparations for art. A shipment of musical instruments may be saluted with fanfare by both the young musicians eager use their new equipment and art students eager to use the packaging materials. The joint unpacking becomes a ceremony, as instruments are carefully extracted and each precious cargo box is hauled into the art room. Art students know that the materials that once secured a cello for the shipping journey are really abstract raw materials with infinite possibilities.

A school art class itself is a busy shipping department, receiving many packages in which to discover highly valuable components. Art students of all ages need to be "deputized" to inspect all cardboard containers and their interior treasures. When paint shipments or a new file cabinet arrives, it is a time for celebration. Unpacking ceremonies can result in harvesting myriad pieces that cannot be bought in an art supply store and, thus, in myriad opportunities for creativity.

Playing with Packaging Materials

Students require little guidance to find imaginative ways to play with stacks of packaging pieces. Unlike some other play materials, packaging offers free form pieces without predetermined uses that require more imaginative effort and thus can offer even more creative rewards.

Foam pieces are easy to puncture, and like shish kabobs on skewers, students can find ways to thread together, carve, and decorate the pieces.

Students freely erect packaging materials into enormous monuments, trophies, and architectural constructs. Enormous Ziggurats of the future rise from shallow boxes stacked into swerving towers.

Amazing framed canvases or fencing materials for prehistoric creatures may lie inside a box. Students can playfully assemble instant landscapes, populated by extraordinary vegetation and creatures. These unexpected landscapes can become motion picture sets ready to be filmed by burgeoning young Spielbergs.

In the process of sorting through unusual forms, students can try them on as ready-to-wear fashion. Clothing inventions and fashion shows that would put *Project Runway* contestants to shame emerge from play with packaging and fabrics.

Students can arrange pieces into changing patterns or maps for imaginary planets. Giant collections of padding pieces can be laid out on any surface into a puzzle-maker's dream.

Students can also enjoy floating their found forms as seascapes on ponds of water (play pools), decorated with paint or shaving cream.

Each of these possible inventions that come straight from observation demonstrate the richness of children's art that comes from playing with packaging materials.

Studying Packaging Materials

Not only are packaging materials good for play and art production, they are good for history lessons and studies in design and in art appreciation. The way packages are arranged, as well as the objects used for packaging, can be a study in form and shape. Students can learn about the history behind developments in packaging or different packaging styles.

For example, eggs used to be shipped in wooden boxes, but now they use paper and Styrofoam containers. Students can be introduced to vintage suitcases, hatboxes, doll trunks, or toy collection cases that are no longer used. The packaging and padding used in old ring cases or antique eyeglass cases provide an interesting study in innovative forms and materials.

Students can also take what they learn about the packaging of the past to imagine and design the packaging of the future. Or they can use packaging materials in their own collections to simply appreciate, which people commonly do with vintage food packaging or bottle carriers. They can collect today's packages to be the vintage objects of tomorrow.

Packaging Lessons

Packaging materials offer a good sampling of contemporary art supplies, art forms, and art designs produced by a global culture that emphasizes easy and fast shipping of goods. Like all lessons about unconventional materials, packaging lessons teach that art supplies required for the art of the future go far beyond the limits of what can simply be purchased in a conventional art supply store.

Play Materials and Collections

To this point, I have addressed different kinds of unconventional art materials and the possible creative uses for them in the play-based classroom. One important discussion about materials remains: creating art through collections.

As a child, my daughter Ana used to enjoy collecting things. Back before digital cameras made the little black film canister practically obsolete, she used them to house a pencil point collection. She saved nail clippings—filed in clear plastic slide pockets—and filled small drawers of parts boxes with clothes tags, washers, and pencil shavings. Teeth she lost were kept in a special jewelry box.

The larger and often hard to classify collections were stored in plastic totes and baskets. These items included such selections as swim goggle cases, golf club cover "socks," and car cup holders. When cleaning her room, Ana often had to defend these holdings and explain why she "needed" a doll case filled with sidewalk pieces. In her art and play, it was clear that her collections were not only important sources for ideas or supplies for creation—in other words, means to an end—but ends in and of themselves, a collection-as-art. To be able to spot and save unusual forms was Ana's art form.

Innovative vision, imaginative seeing, is unique to children's creative behavior. A young child's occupation is to crawl and search for interesting things to pick up. Naturally active observers, children scan and scavenge through the environment, check everywhere, look up and down, survey floors, shelves, and containers as they pocket and curate collections. If allowed to keep all they select, children would have no space to walk in their room. Moving with curious eyes wide open to the world is the most valuable trait of young artists.

As I've noted, supportive parents don't call collections 'junk' but value children's finds as important treasures. Supportive art teachers recognize the value in protecting and welcoming these expressions of curiosity and take children's collections seriously. Art teachers can learn from children playing with their collections and make it a model for art room activities. They can provide an ongoing gallery to display children's collections or institute an intermittent collector's fair where all kids' collections are celebrated.

Opportunities to Collect

Play and art making are most intensely focused when children use their own collections, whether obtained from home or school. The treasures that make up a child's finds are also their favorite forms to arrange, display, and use as art supplies. More inspiring than what adults select for them, a child's collection is complete with personal plans for play ideas. Collecting is an opportunity for young artists to make independent choices and demonstrate their taste and interest.

Collecting is also an environmental treasure hunt, a play that creates excitement about discovery. A challenging hunt through the backyard, schoolyard, or a grocery store is a playful adventure. Spotting something special is a gratifying moment. When an art class is comfortable with fearless collecting, the doors are open for all kinds of unusual and beautiful things to be saved for class. Everyone should be collecting things to premiere in the art class, to show and tell about. The more opportunities that parents and teachers provide for collecting, the more rewards students reap from the hunt.

Displaying Collections

Once children have begun to assemble their collections, teachers can continue to encourage them by making those collections public. Having students share their latest collection is an effective way to start each art class and gives students confidence in their personal choices. The sharing can be as informal as having children empty their pockets and lunchboxes to show and tell about recent collections.

Or the sharing can be more formal, done in designated displays. In this way, welcoming children's precious objects may involve designing a display case or pop-up collection case that can be a traveling museum. Some students might want to make illustrated brochures to catalogue a collection. Arranging books is a way to turn a display creation into an art project. Stamp and sticker books, albums for Band-Aid, Post-its, and stationary collections all require careful and creative organizing. Making albums or other student constructed showcases can be regular activities in an art room that hosts children's collections and their display. The playful planning and development of a display for precious collections is in itself a wonderful children's art.

The main thing is for teachers to be sure to provide places and times to display the collections. Special trays and folding tables can be dedicated to displays. Empty fish tanks, secondhand jewelry boxes, vintage tin playhouses can all be used as art class museums for new installations. Children showcase their collections in playful ways that are unlike traditional museum displays, in set-ups reminiscent of their doors, corkboards, and shelves at home. Constantly refurnished playhouses or toy refrigerators can have festive grand openings to celebrate new collections.

Using Collections

While not all children will want to use the items from a collection for play or art projects, some might see their finds as possible art supplies. Student collectors can share their wares and ask their peers to transform them, to try wearing them as disguises, or to explore them as building blocks. Other object collections, such as different clothes clips, unusual hair curlers, or an ice cream cone collection, may be used as play figures. Encouraging class trades and auctions can add another element of fun to using collections in the classroom. Students can "bid" for the items in other students' collections or practice bartering in order to get new art tools and canvases. Or, they can make standing orders, asking classmates to keep an eye out for a certain kind of treasure to complete a long-term collection.

Do as the Teacher Does

Art teachers should also constantly build up their collection of amazing objects to pass around for students to hold and play with. Antique play blocks, amazing pull toys, vintage game boards, or extraordinary toy carrying cases are great art for them to experience first hand. When an art teacher is an enthusiastic collector, he or she inspires others to collect. The size of the collection, its rarity, or its monetary value is not important. An art teaching collection can be modest, consisting of one or two significant or favorite objects. It can also be used as an inspiration for a class collection. Maybe the teacher can bring in a collection of unusual socks and ask students to do the same. Building a collection together is a good way to ensure students understand the value of their collecting impulses. Collections show basic art values, such as an early commitment to the love of unusual and beautiful things. Children collecting and encountering great collections is the museum experience art classes can provide daily.

Lessons From Experience

As a child of immigrants, I learned not to depend on toy stores or art supply stores to find what I needed. There were so many interesting American supplies that were available. I collected shiny shopping bags for space suits. There were plastic Baggies, metallic wallpaper samples, and amazing burger wraps to build anything. I became an avid art supply shopper at neighborhood yard sales and secondhand stores. I developed an early appreciation for McDonald's and the Dollar Store as the best places to find future art supplies, used to dress and equip my play figures. I started using Kleenex, Scotch tape, and plastic hair curlers to create play settings for cereal box prizes.

My own experiences have confirmed for me that life imitates art and vice versa, and we can learn from both, as art teachers and guides. That is why I want to use this section to share some other anecdotes from my life and observations that highlight the importance of viewing the world as your art store and in recognizing the creative possibilities from using unconventional materials in play and art.

Playful Shopping

Children are masters of spotting free art supplies in a store or on the street and intuitively identifying a slew of ideas for their use. No adult gets as excited as Emilie in turning a corner and finding a display of free paint sample cards. She seldom takes one of any find. Long produce bags and ties are saved and loaded up in bunches for later creative play. Emilie passes by the floral aisle and helps herself to several clear triangular bouquet bags, blowing them up and tying their corners to different openings on the shopping cart. Emilie later patiently admires the creations of stock clerk artists building a mound of apples and waits until there are enough blue fruit paddings and folding partitions available from the apple crates to choose from.

During a recent car trip, my granddaughter turned a truck stop into an art store. She made the rounds through the unusual conglomeration of items meant to pep up the tired traveler. She thoughtfully crisscrossed seemingly random displays, filling her basket with such items as Magic Noodles, Glow sticks, colored glue sticks, and dinosaur eggs. She found amazing illustrated Band-Aids, new duct tape patterns, and added a new color to her paint collection of day glow-sparkly nail polishes.

What is labeled and sold as a traditional art supplies tends to be the least attractive to Emilie's fancy-free shopping. Among her recent finds that may revolutionize the future of art, Emilie located interesting canvases in a beauty supply wholesale store, and the most promising tools at a restaurant supply outlet.

The game I play with Emilie, and my art classes, is to rename every store an art supply store and treat it as such. Parents and teachers can elevate all shopping to an exciting environmental search, looking for new canvases, art tools, paints, and items to build and perform with. A flat tire may lead to a tire store, but also an unforgettable experience to dream of new art tools and surfaces, printing and playing devices. A candy store or a fabric store can be entered as an art supply store for testing and idea shopping.

Playful Repurposing

Old, used stuff may not seem precious or expensive, but it yields a wealth of new thoughts about what could be used and useful in making things. Unreservedly pulling down items from the shelves at a Habitat for Humanity store, Emilie puts some wooden stair railings, floor tiles, and bricks into her cart. She wants help with a gently used, but nicely framed, white cabinet door. She talks about painting on some of her pieces while gluing together others. Being free to shop in any store for art supplies extends the idea of where art might live or come from. Emilie's notion of what is "proper" as art supplies or art objects has no bounds while shopping.

Students can be encouraged to take weekly field trips to stores in the community (some trips they may already take with their parents), but with a new license to investigate and play in the aisles in preparing for the art class. With some parent education, visits to the florist, tire store, or ice cream shop can be prime opportunities to study colors or surfaces, gather printing ideas, or start a new collection of interesting objects. Art teachers can promote this kind of playful shopping and enlist students as procurers of art supplies by giving students a list of fun stores where touching is free and sampling is possible. Stores that allow browsing, touching, and playful hands may include thrift shops, dollar stores, pet stores, or produce aisles of a supermarket. Art education is teaching students to look for ideas, feel unusual surfaces, fill empty pockets, and think of art in whatever store they visit. Discoveries can be encouraged by an exciting show and tell, regular sharing sessions, and debriefings in the art class.

Playing at the Store

Not only is the store a place where children can obtain unconventional materials for art, but it is also a place where they create art. During another supermarket trip, Emilie becomes the stock clerk artist, using a bounty of bananas for a fruit construction project to build while her mom is busy at the pharmacy section. The rise of the circular tower attracts the attention of many observers, admirers of child art, and a few critics. When the young artist runs out of bananas, Emilie reaches into the next tray to balance apples on her spiraling yellow foundation. The next day, I carry bananas to my art class and photographs of her construction project to celebrate her as a shopping artist and encourage my students to do the same.

When Emilie was very young and a restrained passenger in a shopping cart, she was expected to keep her hands inside. Now that she's older and allowed to get out of the cart, it is expected that shopping will include touching, sampling, and posing, as a way to building experiences and resulting art ideas. When the "don't touch," "don't pocket," "don't save" mottoes are relaxed by adults, or even encouraged by parents, students engage in valuable art plays in public places.

Playing Outdoors

Growing up after World War II in Budapest, my childhood playground was outdoors. Among the rubble, there were plenty of toys to be discovered. With no shortage of bent metal items and ball bearings from abandoned vehicles, wheeled toys like my special scooters could be assembled. Plenty of wires could be pulled from the debris to fashion soldiers and cars. Life without toys made the environment a provider of options, and we found and converted what we needed.

Years later when I arrived in America to settle near Brooklyn's Brighton Beach, I found a friend and a field of dreams that provided endless play supplies. Brighton was not the dreamy Mediterranean that I learned about in picture books. Unkempt during the winter months, our Atlantic Ocean beach was a dump. For my American friend and me, who could not communicate through language, Brighton was a happy dump that provided endless possibilities. We spoke through the things we found, traded, and built on the beach. Many years passed, and my friend and I both entered the art school of The Cooper Union. To this day we still talk about art lessons on the beach and the opportunities we discovered there.

The fact that both Dennis and I ended up teaching art in the same poor industrial school district of the city was a blessing. With a degree in art, and a résumé as Brighton Beach Explorers, we found little difficulty in adjusting to the elementary schools that provided few art supplies. We immediately embarked on teaching students what we knew best, turning the yields of streets and factories into great supplies. Students looked around and provided the materials, and we offered the space and support to make the most amazing things. We encouraged students to share their stories of discoveries and to keep material diaries and sketches, to come as well prepared to the art class as their new art teachers.

Dennis and I repeatedly told our stories of adventures on Brighton Beach. To encourage creative thinking, and to play the job of parents and art teachers, is to help students find their own beaches, dumps, or sidewalks for supply shopping. We provided the shopping bags, shopping carts, and the trust in what young artists pick out as being valuable. Students need to feel that their choices are worthy of keeping, that their finds are welcome at home and in the art room.

Play Materials and the Future of Art

Art of the past required a different kind of material preparation. When art was confined inside picture frames, art education meant learning skills to create illusions of reality on a flat surface. Tricks of perspective, shading, and design principles were taught to create illusions of a three-dimensional world. For this purpose, uniform art materials were bought, and later ordered from catalogues or listed as required art supplies on hand-outs.

Today, students stare at screens instead of looking into a picture frame. They watch the world on TV, capture reality on phone screens, or play with virtual reality in video games. Museums project video art on walls, and teachers show the outside world on Smart Boards. Art Education places emphasis on creating images on computer screens, and the supply most often requested is technology.

But, what does art look like after the illusion of the framed canvas is removed from museum walls? What will art be like after screens that have monopolized our viewing? Well, there are important hints . . . instead of frames, museums now allow artists to work directly on the wall. Exhibits often feature real environmental objects, like placing a dumpster in a museum. Staples and suitcases, cars, and car parts are used as artist's materials. Beyond paint and technology many artists are back to what young children have always used in their creative playing: sticks and environmental finds, stones and objects found in streets and stores. Moving from illusions on canvases and screens, children and artists are looking for and playing with real objects and materials.

Consequently, change is necessary in school art, change that comes from impulses many of us already have or had when we were children. A population used to looking into a rectangular world needs to again become aware of the environment, real objects and real materials represented in contemporary life. We need a pass to play again, to get our hands back into sand, leaves, and water, to hunt for treasures and make the world our art store. Only through these changes will we begin to uncover the infinite possibilities waiting in the future of art.

5

MOVEMENT IN PLAY AND ART

FIGURE 5.0 Rehearsing playful hands and bodies helps children to discover new ways to hold and dance with art tools.

Children's art is motivated by all kinds of play, and even playful movements can be a source for their artistic expressions. This chapter describes art rooms where active learners, action viewers, and fast-paced players create or experience art through movement. Instead of designing spectator events for students based on passive consumption, the chapter suggests ways to initiate art room experiences where creative movement is an art and participation in movement play also inspires works in traditional art media.

Art and Inspiring Performances

Most adults need coffee to get them going in the morning, and they often lag until they get it. Children wake up running and ready to conquer the world. Aliza, at two years old, does not walk; she runs through the house checking each room and what's going on. She moves across rooms with excitement, leaving marks, spills, dropping things on the floor, and occasionally colliding with furnishing. After a bumpy ride on the stairs, Aliza pauses to nurse a "booboo"; then she continues moving and exploring, excited about all the possibilities everywhere. She climbs on an old sofa to test its springy action and catapults herself to a higher chair to jump off.

Spotting food on the breakfast table, Aliza applies the brakes. She takes her place at the table to animate every object within reach. Between courses, she moves to the beats set by a busy refrigerator: the opening and closing of doors, warning beeps, ice cubes crunching and tumbling into glasses, and a buzzing compressor. Her response is an ode to an electrical machine: a two-part dance, standing on the dining room chair. Following breakfast, there will be hoops and slides and acrobatics in the pool, as she continues a day of stirring artistic action. Parents and teachers take note! Like Aliza, most children are great improvisers and inventors of movement adventures. From the time they wake up, through outdoor playing to bedtime ablutions, children dance through their day, dancing, acting, exploring, and essentially creating performance art through play movements.

Movement in the Art Room

When I was a child attending elementary school in Vienna, I carried a standard-issue brown leather briefcase that included, among other items, a soft, ballet-style gym shoe. My art teacher required that students put on soft shoes for exercising before making art. On tiptoes, we would lift our bodies upward, raising our hands, before bending low and deep toward the floor. We rotated our heads, necks, and arms, moved every part of our body down to the fingers. In this classroom, exercising was not only a way to counteract the effects of draining sitting postures, but it was also a way to prepare for and celebrate the art to come during the class.

Herr Manfreda, the art teacher, recognized that drawing shapes and lines in art required different moves than penmanship and writing. To break from the rest of the school day, Manfreda's students used calisthenics to release tension and as a prelude to drawing. Nothing in Manfreda's strict art class resembled play, and after exercising we sat at rigid tables again to work on precise drawings of apples on graph paper.

As a Manfreda student, now art teacher, I also turn to movement to differentiate art from the rest of school. However, these are movements based in play that pay homage to an important children's art form. Movement provides a playful search engine with which students of all ages can find art, and it takes art out of chairs and away from desks. Through imaginative moves that span the art room floor, students dance and rehearse using their bodies or other objects and tools before and during art making. Movement play helps children discover their passions, sparks imaginations, and promotes their natural powers of creativity. However, most art education texts and classes are still divided into drawing, painting, and other traditional media and neglect movement. Adults would do well to remedy this omission and foster children's natural physical creativity by offering support, time, and space.

The New Art

When children move, it is often an experiment, and no two performances are alike. Their physical expressions are an exhibit that not only expresses creativity but also invites it from the audience of other children who are welcome to join in, experiment with their own movements. Thus, the audience becomes the performer, and the performer can now watch and learn from the audience or continue to perform. The lines between passive appreciator and active artist blur and bring to light new possibilities for art.

This is just one example of the ways that the art world can benefit from watching the imaginative expressions of children. And the contemporary art world has begun to confirm what children have always demonstrated in practice: that art can be physical, a performance. Art is a moving act that can be explored through anything from drawing tools to Slinkys. Playing as a way to art can focus on creative body moves, moving tools and objects creatively, or even moving audiences. Following the lead of children like Aliza, artists today often embrace movement as an integral part of artistic expression. As exhibits move art off museum walls and pedestals and into new spaces, movement becomes a new art medium.

Nurturing the Physical Artist

When Elmo plays, children stop. The same goes for watching television and playing on an iPad, which might engage their mind but not their bodies. Such activities turn potential movement inventors into passive audiences who rely on action created and performed by others for entertainment. As long as children move, they keep investigating and inventing, transferring energy to playing with all their found objects. Emilie, at age nine, still plays through movement, and her moves are relatively unhampered by writing or routines. She hip hops and invents new moves each minute; she freely propels objects or paint across any surface. However, most children by this age have become inactive audiences, giving up performing to technology that moves for them.

Art rooms can be instrumental in promoting students' movement art, including variations on hopping, leaping, climbing, jumping, and playing with moving objects, balls, and action figures. Creative moving widens opportunities to spark the interests and passions of children. Action playing is vital in getting kids excited about learning and exploring. Students discover ideas in their active plays on which to build art projects about what they imagine. When children can creatively move in an art class, they are observing and learning from their own acts and the acts of others. Playful actions and movements are ways to tinker and test objects and environments in a lively setting of imaginative experimentation. That is why the contemporary art class has to be designed to keep student bodies unreservedly playing and moving. Lifeless bodies cannot perform creatively. Thus, art teachers have to find ways to make the art class a moving experience.

Art in Movement

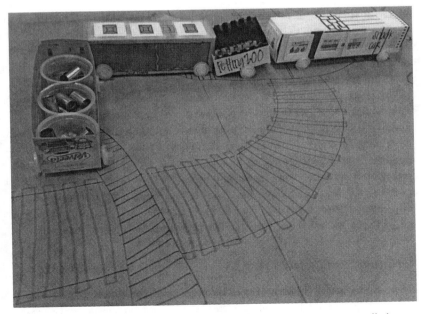

FIGURE 5.1 Play art can be pulled and pushed, steered, or remote controlled.

Children live in spontaneously moving bodies, as playful movers of things. Their art emerges not only through drawings and paintings but also through a variety of movements that can thrive in an art class. Movement play is a unique art that resembles traditional arts such as dance, acting, improvisational theater, or puppetry and can be considered the origins of pantomime, shadow-theater, or circus arts.

Children's performances are moving scenarios with objects and toys. Young children are always putting on a show for adults, and while some parents may call these shows silly acts, really they are imaginative improvisations and ingenious staging ideas. Play movements support imaginative actions outdoors or in an art room, and the art teacher can be a leader in initiating playful moves, actions, and performances where students try things out and evoke imaginative states.

Taking Notes

Observing children in movement play and noting their performance inventions can be useful for art teachers. I take notes on a napkin, which then spill over onto placemats, while observing Emilie's moving art of dancing sugar packet and spinning chopsticks. Her play passes the time before dinner arrives at the table. For me, it represents an exciting opportunity to learn. This summer, I sketched my napkin notes at the Ulster County Fair (N.Y.). The movements depicted in sack races, rope pulls, and sideshows abound in materials that make the start of any art class a moving event. From the notes I make, I translate my observations into school art sessions. The following are examples of some of the art room movement plays that I have noted during my examinations.

Jump Play

Children love to be superheroes. Shortly after conquering walking, they discover they can jump. From here, it's just a short leap before children discover the superhero within, and observing a child with a cape discovering they can fly is an artistic occasion. Art classes can challenge students to maintain their delight with basic moving acts. An erect art class can try out ski jumps, ballet leaps, or frog hopping. With stick horses, pogo sticks, and jump ropes, students can expand their jumping repertoire and perform artistic demonstrations. Take out your napkins or placemats to contemplate the supportive grounds, environments, and props an art room can provide for jumping meets.

Power Tool Play

Now, letting children play with power tools might be a safety hazard, but letting them be power tools is an exercise in creative fun. There are plenty of exciting tools that children can imitate to get them moving imaginatively. Ask them to become a can opener, a toaster, or a multi-speed blender. Stand aside as students plug themselves into a wall to become a drill or unplug themselves for a cordless hedge trimmer. They can be a lawn mower, a hair dryer, anything that suits their creative impulses at that moment.

Pose Play

While it might seem counterintuitive, asking students to freeze in creative poses requires thoughtful movement. They can replicate a famous painting, pose like a Greek sculpture, get up on a chair like it's a pedestal and interpret art through their bodies. They can even create new sculptures that have yet to be imagined.

Marathon Moves

Children often encounter *No Running* signs. A pool deck or school hallways declares this favorite activity off-limits. Runners, however, cannot be kept down, and art classes can honor their racing impulses. For an art class 5K I've observed, numbers were made for the competitors to wear and the course colorfully outlined on the floor. In the race, play figures or horses participated, and even art tools raced for the title of fastest and longest drawing. The art class can be envisioned as a racetrack, a stadium, or a pool for fast paced movers. Some marathons can be recorded on papers, while others can be filmed. In smaller spaces, relay races can accommodate the actions of runners.

Stunt Driving

I've witnessed matchbox cars and found objects such as styled erasers turned into stunt cars and lined up behind student designed checkered flags. From starting gates cars lift off into the air, looping, and barely touching different class surfaces in fancy driving demonstrations. Climbing up the slopes of toilet paper and sliding down adding machine tape, students negotiated tricky courses for stunt runs. An art class camera crew captured each exciting moment of the event.

Robot Play

In one art class, students were welcomed with an open suitcase revealing its contents of old game controllers (a Goodwill collection). After students warmed up to the song "Walk Like an Egyptian," they became robots that were wound up and fueled with a pretend hose. Each robot partnered with another student who then pressed the robot student's starter button. The student controllers commanded their robot partners' moves using the game controllers. One student suggested a school dance for robots, and it was filmed as a special art room event.

Sketches from the Carousel

In a constant search for children's movement arts, I find myself at the park, my napkin sketches piling up. I observe children not riding the carousel but forming one in a circle, acting as their own carousel figures. They laugh, change poses, and spin around. The body creatures they create are as interesting as the world of the Swiss art troupe, Mummenschanz. With enthusiasm, I related the story and showed the illustrations to the art class.

As always, the students edited and improved on each idea with an abundance of original suggestions. One memorable version was a flashlight show in which students posed as monsters in a circle, and used the rich art room flashlight collection to project circling shadows on the screen of an enclosure formed by hanging tracing papers from the ceiling. Changing color monsters floated on the 3D screen housing the performing carousel artists. This is a great example of how students in an art class can pose and pretend to be anything, how body plays can be imaginatively staged with minimal props.

Clowning Around

Clowns, or clowning, are typically punished in school. From an adult's perspective, it seems like fooling around, but it's really behavior that gives one permission to be playful enough to attempt silly moves. Encouraging clowning can start with silly things to do. Ripping apart the foam inserts from a set of outdoor cushions is a fun and playful act that leads to more creativity. One student wears the foam, posing as a muscle man. Another clown juggles the foam and adds an extra nose to soft body parts. They find ways to stuff their clothing and balance the foam on their heads. Each clown, magician, and actor can create recordings of progressing events.

Animators From Within

Just like on a playground, children enjoy moving through a tunnel, a plastic pipe, or a covered slide navigating their bodies into the unknown. In the art class, students discuss the fun of playing in pillowcases and reshaping sleeping bags from the inside. Moving inside sacks, large sheets of paper, large shopping bags, or inhabiting a wide tube or a cardboard box allows for a variety of moving performances.

Running the Show

Many children like to take charge and perform roles that direct the movements of other children or of objects. Putting dollies to bed is a universal theme for pretend parents. Creative young fashion designers can organize beach towel fashion shows that give them a chance to not only explore creative draping but also direct the models on this runway to move unlike any traditional fashion models. Students pretending to be dance teachers, animators, or conductors can teach play figures to creatively move. When a student is play-acting the choreographer, all surfaces in an art room are a stage for tools and objects to perform. In the art class, students at play are able to use their bodies and the simplest forms they animate with unrestrained abandon.

Art and Movement Play

I Hate Rules!

Danielle wanted to know why she couldn't take her American Girl doll, named Molly, to dance class. "When I dance with Molly, everybody smiles and applauds." I concurred that my granddaughter Danielle moved her doll with amazing innovation and that she was indeed a wonderful choreographer. However, her mom explained that the dance school has rules. Danielle replied, "I hate rules!"

Students of all ages need to dance, move, and create things without rules; the opportunity to do things their way without starting with a list of how-tos challenges creators. Art teaching is providing opportunities for inventive movers to act as performance artists and break the rules.

Playing with objects that move without laying down rules is an essential contribution to using movement as a tool for invention. Opening classroom floors and spaces to pretend performances in art class animates bodies and imaginations. Below, I provide some examples of the simple toys used in our Centers for Creative Art Teaching that others can use to reshape the child's visionary world. Moves with everything from instruments to ribbons, confetti to toilet paper rolls, and streamers to bubbles promote performance art for inventive souls that hate rules.

Dancing to a Saxophone

A toy saxophone is our grandchildren's boom box and fancy music machine. The colorful toy is twistable and can be shaped into a trumpet, a sax, or abstract instruments. Lots of buttons correspond to sounds and lively, compact musical passages that make everyone in the room want to dance. The musical toy officially belongs to granddaughter Aliza, but it frequently brings an entire art class to their twisting and turning feet. There is no need to rehearse or demonstrate proper steps. The saxophone sound just enters bodies, taking them in all directions. Students of all ages can move to the sax, children's records, blenders, toy synthesizers, or party noisemakers. In an art class, students become movement inventors and dance their way.

Rocking the Flea Market Toy Guitar

Rock and rollers are never too young or to old to perform. Students can create impromptu stages and sets to wow their audiences with their compositions, or they can use the guitars as other movement props, dancing and moving with them like Gene Kelly with his umbrella in "Singin' in the Rain."

Noodles in the Air

What spurs original movements at home, or in the art class, are often simple forms that might not even seem like toys or props. A package arrives at home containing foam noodle packing material, and children are wound up for a moving celebration. During the invention festival, the white forms get dumped and flow like confetti through the air. The room fills with laughter and creative actions. A fiesta of movements can be recreated in the art room wrapped in such joyful creative materials. The flight of noodles and their landing leads to mini stacks and mounds, play foods, and snowy inventions that reshape the room and the students' moves.

Playing with Balloons

Just taking possession of a classroom set of large and resilient helium balloons makes students float with excitement. With all the different balloons, the class looks like a hot air balloon regatta. Individual handlers discover their art as they attach their imagination and moves to the balloons' flight.

The Bubble Machine

A gurgling, bright yellow device that looks like a small television spews out thousands of different bubbles. With the press of a button, an art teacher can step anywhere in the room and release an impressive array of floating spheres that land on a nose or merge into a bubble shower. Freestyle, or with an umbrella, students move to duck or juggle the avalanche heading their way. Bubble dancing is an exciting and always fresh art form that washes the face and stimulates performing and painting inspirations.

Pool Play

Wearing swim goggles in art class indicates fun. Wet paper towels or a tape drawing of a pool on the floor invites jumping into the refreshing water and enjoying water movement play. Blowing a lifeguard whistle signals that the pool is open. To start the water play, class suggestions can be helpful: "Let's get in the water," or "Hold your nose and take a deep breath as we go under." Students perform water ballets, practice diving forms, play Marco Polo, pretend to be submarines, and invent games. They gracefully demonstrate how water and movement art combine.

Winter Play

The sheet of ice applied to the art room floor may just be a large drop cloth, but young skaters don't mind. On skates that are imaginary or made from pop sticks or markers taped to shoes that record each moving event, they rehearse their fantastic moves. For winter skiers, there are always the slopes; drapings of adding machine tape with loops and curves, and breathtaking descents that inspire ski slaloms, fancy jumps, and invented sports such as ski dancing. With minimum props and open fields for imaginations to roam, any art room becomes a wintery field of moving dreamers.

Art Room Highways and Speedways

U-drive, U-steer it, U-handle the turns! With a collection of pot cover steering wheels, students in an art class obtain a license to drive. Taking the wheel of a makeshift family car, grand-prix racer, or fire engine on call, play movers suggest the speed, terrain, or circumstances of the emergency. Riding on chairs, magic carpets, or moon rovers, and taking off on skateboards or rolling suitcases allows a vast range of daring movements to be attempted. For drivers, building their own moving toys inspires additional art development opportunities. Such movement play gives students a new perspective of office chairs, storage boxes, refrigerator movers, roller skates, and all things on wheels as valuable chassis on which to mobilize their imaginations.

Rousing Movements

To play and dance with broomsticks, brushes, or dolls requires freedom from rubrics, requirements, and guidelines for what to do and how to do it. Young artists require the maximum opportunity to invent moves and move their own way at home and in the art class. That is why explorations in an art class should encourage galloping, skiing, dancing, and driving and consider students' movement innovations as play that results in art and a way to appreciate art by stirring moves. Also, the class should provide showcases to preserve the talents of young movement inventors. Young children can create a "show a minute," calling parents or other children to see it, distributing tickets. Pretend shows are an essential part of an art program.

This is all part of how adults can inspire creative playing before presenting lessons that draw boundaries around art.

Action Toys and Movement

Last section, I described ways to use certain objects in motion play. However, some toys are already intended to inspire motion. Motion toys promote a variety of ways to stir a child's hands, mind, and body. Experiencing and creating exciting movements with motion toys provides a vast resource of ideas that translate

FIGURE 5.2 A skateboarder, made by active players, demonstrates action art.

to dramatic moves over art surfaces. Parents and teachers can offer children toys like those I suggest below that allow young artists to explore movements in playing and art making.

Tops

Sitting on the kitchen floor and watching wonderfully decorated old tin toy tops spin is a memorable grandparent moment. The tops in my collection are mostly those made in the 1940s–60s by Chein. There are also toys from different countries and continents that spin, displaying a universal fascination with the humming of dancing tops. One regular crowd-pleaser in the collection is a tin ballerina in a black tutu made by Marx Toys around 1935. Whether it's at home or in an art class, children cannot wait for a turn to launch a top on their own. What could be more fun than being on the art room floor and starting a class with exciting movements inspired by spinning toys? Watching students play along as they watch the movie *Tops Spinning*, a mid-century film by Charles Eames (easily accessible on YouTube) is like a good piano accompaniment to a silent Chaplin film.

Once children have learned the movements that such toys offer them, they can create their own variations on the theme and take the movement to new levels of creativity. To warm up for a lesson, the entire class can stand and spin. Students can extend their moves with streamers or by unfurling toilet paper to make a more dramatic dance. While in rotation, the dreams of children spin into great art inventions, trying a bike wheel as a top, and later accessorizing it with drawing tools on board. Spinning pushpins dipped in color trace different spiraling paths. Drawings and paintings can follow the spinning path, suggesting new processes and ways to make art.

Hula-Hoops

Henry Moore and other adult artists tell the story of starting the day with a walk, to stimulate ideas for the day while moving. An art class can also awaken the creative spirit with active moving, with plays and laughter. Hula-Hoops are another great tool to evoke spinning performances and gyrating bodies as rotating art. Testing vintage hoops and trying out the latest light-up, liquid-and-confetti-filled models brings students together in a joyful experience that leads to many inventions.

Children make valuable connections between their motion toys and new ways to use them, while inventing new art. For example, hoops suggest new handles for art tools, when markers or brushes are attached. Instead of brushing a painting, a hoop with brush attachments allows for bold circular movements leaving bright paths of swirling colors. Students explore Hula-Hoops as canvas stretchers, to playfully rotate and set into motion a color wheel. Moving the canvas during the act of painting opens up many new ways to paint. Others try the hoop as a canvas itself, to paint, decorate with duct tape, or use as a loom to stretch great round weavings.

Yo-Yos

Students enjoy watching yo-yo artistry, witnessing the skills and inventiveness possible with a simple toy classic. They also enjoy creating yo-yo artistry by adding tails, wings, paint, and other attachments to expand on the attributes of a beloved flying sculpture. Students can explore the physical sensation of the toy hanging from their hand, swinging like a pendulum, sleeping, or walking. They can invent dances in space and on paper in homage to their string explorations moving up and down in bold new angles and configurations. Watching the yo-yo line twist, swirl, and shoot out straight can provide inspiring lessons about lines. After yo-yo plays in an art class, no one in class draws the same way again.

Toys on Wheels

With wheels, children's art gains speed and a sense of freedom and independence. Students can test moving easels and canvases and try painting and drawing over paper or fabric-wrapped platforms, such as a sliding car mechanic's dolly, appliance moving platforms, or skateboards. All kinds of antique toys on wheels, such as vintage toy shopping carts, classic scooters, and bicycles can inspire new moves and innovative sculptural constructions. Making wheels available for any school art project adds a new dimension to painting, or sculpture that can be pushed or pulled, mounted, navigated, or piloted for a ride. Skateboards provide an instant cart for an art room or a pull-push toy chassis for all forms of rolling artistry.

Remote-Controlled Toys

After playing with remote-controlled toys in class, art tools speed up and fast forward at a new pace. Drawings become longer, more rhythmic, swaying, twisting, and turning in surprising changes and directions. Playing with motion toys teaches young artists new moves and flight patterns. Through remote-controlled helicopters and stunt cars, drawing lines learn to fly. Inspired by the free voyages and "footprints" left by remote-controlled toys on the ground or in the air, students can find new ways to direct art tools over art surfaces.

Tech Toys and Movement

Play is not what it used to be. Technology has changed children's attention span, toy preferences, and the way children move with toys. Aliza touches her Mozart Cube and chuckles and swings to the classics. A little squeeze to the toe of her red stuffed animal Elmo, and he joins her doing the Moonwalk. She sits before a palace rearranging the furniture. The oven rings, buzzes, sings, accompanying Elmo, who is still going strong, now reciting the alphabet backwards. With little effort and small moves, pushing buttons, squeezing triggers and controls, toys provide entertaining moves and sounds that can act as modern instruments that inspire performance art.

FIGURE 5.3 The play set-up for a design lab explores the new in figurative objects and dwellings.

Tech Toys—Sounds and Moving

Yes, programmed toys like video games can be ignored in the art class, but that doesn't mean tech toys can't supplement other toy movement play. For example, "playing" a drum set that only requires pushing a button doesn't mean that the beats can't accompany an impromptu concert on traditional play instruments. The tech-based sounds add a different kind of resonance and allow for different kinds of orchestration that encourage imaginative approaches to music and sound. It's also just as fun for children to dance to tech-based musical instruments that create the music for them as it is to dance to actual toy pianos, metal drums, or play accordions. The key is to get them moving but also to get them thinking about experiences in new ways and get them combining media for new creative endeavors.

Do We Have Batteries in the House?

Vintage battery toys are like moving sculptures that delight anyone in the art room. These creaky, slow moving tin toys, painted with interesting graphics, require large batteries to be awakened from deep sleep. Once on the move, they project light shows, simple elegant moves, and levitating acts. Radar Robot fascinates everyone with a light up television chest, smoking head, and planets floating above its head. The Big Band consists of marching soldiers led by a large rolling drummer. Once started, students are eager to follow with their own improvised march. An elephant blowing bubbles and a monkey playing drums demonstrate simple mechanics that produce sounds with clever movements. They suggest a style of action and pace that is fun for children to join. Choreographers require inspiration, and for young movement designers, old toys provide many moves to mimic or use as a basis for experimentation.

Wind Them Up

Other predecessors to high tech toys are the wind-up toys. With a collection of old wind-up toy keys spread out on a school desk, first the toys on the table perform and then students are wound up to join the celebration. Mid-century spinning ballerinas, revolving carousels, winding roller coasters made from beer cans during WWII are beautiful sculptures in motion. They leave audiences of students of all ages wanting to buzz and twirl. Students laugh as they try to imitate and predict the next movement sequence before it happens.

Video Gaming in the Art Class

Young art students come to class with amazing new skill sets learned from following and controlling fast-action video games. Our new artists have fast vision and agile hands to create high-speed works in all media. With 3D images, fast-paced video game action, and amazing sound effects, movement has become an important means of interacting with technology. As students volley back and forth with technology, they get to be more in sync with its speed and moves, and creativity and invention become the means of engagement.

The Wii and Art

Twister in the art class used to loosen student bodies through playful contortions. Now, the Wii opens up a whole new world to art room playing and moving. Playing with the Wii may not be performance art, but it allows a new art world of movement and images to be envisioned. From action eyelids to tapping feet, every inch of our selves can be used to control images. This new high-speed remote interaction with images and bodies has changed children's art and what children can imagine doing in an art room. Art teachers may not have much experience and may not know all the answers for the Wii-playing generation, but by using it in the art class students increase their facility in engaging technology with artistic production.

All That Glitters

You can make art on a flat screen, but there is nothing like plain old glitter to stoke a young artist's flame. This summer, granddaughter Danielle was offered carte blanche at the art supply store. She filled her cart with glitter in all colors and incarnations. Danielle savored her purchases in the car, and could not wait to go to work. Stirring and pouring glitter over plates and in plastic cups, Danielle smeared her magic potions onto different boxes and nature finds. She danced around happily testing and altering the mixes with her fingers and sticks. There were plenty of video games and talking dollhouse furnishings on our porch to play with all summer. However, Danielle sought more freedom of movement, which resulted in art derived from her spirited messing and playing with the mixtures of glitter she cooked up. Tech toys needn't be banned or feared in the art classroom, but they can only go so far as creative inspirations to satisfy the art spirit the way free movement can.

Traditional Tools and Movement

The grandchildren's departure from our home means the conclusion of another summer. My wife and I embark on a massive cleanup ritual to the tune of, "If you buy them glitter again, I'll kill you!" This cry reflects enduring conflict

FIGURE 5.4 Paper conveyor belts for the endless doodling of fresh ideas.

between adults and children whose celebratory explorations leave deposits of sparkling glittery mess everywhere.

Children use traditional art materials and tools like toys, enthusiastically playing with them. They play with glitter or brushes exploring and improvising, trying new moves. Granddaughter Aliza plays with brushes, finding pleasure in stirring them around in a water container. She dips them in paint and shakes out colors over everything. Painting for children is a dance with tools and colors, lively moving, laughing, and engaging with the resulting paths, drips, and puddles. Children's moves animate art making and help to find new ways to make art.

Moving Art Tools Playfully

Playful actions with materials and tools are always important to start art investigations. In art class, students can dance and move with glitter, brushes, paints, canvas, paper, glue, and other traditional materials. Action interludes or preludes to any art project only increase the opportunities to improvise with creative techniques. The following examples illustrate how traditional art tools like a paintbrush can be used to promote movement in the creation of play art.

> Dry brushing means playing with the brush before getting down to painting. Using actual brushes, they can paint in the air, experiment with strange strokes that use the whole body, or get a running start to fling imaginary paint off a dry brush. Imaginary or "magic" brushes are great ways to "paint" in taboo areas, like a museum, or forbidden surfaces like living room walls and school hallways.
>
> Wet brushing can keep brush moves inventive without the distraction of picture making. Amusing brushes of a substantial scale such as mops, dusters, toilet brushes can be dipped in water for moving over indoor floors or concrete outside. Plastic watering cans and a myriad of other items can be used as wet brushes over concrete walkways to rehearse painting movements.
>
> Well-dressed brushes wrapped in foils and giftwrap and handled with white gloves can be asked to dance. Any classroom canvas can serve as the dance floor. Acting as a ballerina, hip-hop dancer, or figure skater, an artist moving with a brush in hand can score high marks.

Action Plays with Glitter

Glitter, plus a child's playful movements, yields a host of inventions in art making, like the following examples.

> Children can create a new dance craze, twirling and winding their arms and bodies while dropping glitter over a large canvas that has been prepped with glue.

Using a rolled-up paper funnel to toss glitter over a surface lets students make a glitter dance with their hands instead of their bodies and demonstrates a lively way to apply other media.

A child's carefree stirring of glitter and glue in different containers is an exciting way to wind up any painting act. They can then smear the glitter-glue on loaves of foam or carpet samples.

Teachers can substitute many materials for glitter to encourage fun movements in an art class.

Freedom Play

As long as children are allowed to play with all tools and supplies freely, students will find new ways to make art. To activate tools and enliven tool users, there needs to be freedom to animate anything as an art tool and to move it everywhere.

Art tools can be used to create new patterns of movement by being attached to Slinkys, flexible vintage television antennas, and baseball gloves, or inserted into flexible hoses or the spout of a teapot. Long, short, or flexible tool extensions suggest new tool handling ideas. Art tools can be wrapped or attached to anything from teeth and toes, shoes and horse shoes, garden tools or kitchen tools, opening the doors to new and active tool handling ideas. Here are a few more examples of ways to engage traditional tools in unusual movement play.

It's high noon, and drawing tools are pulled from a student's belt. The winner of this duel can be the first one to complete a picture of a newly imagined sheriff's star.

Drawing pencils marked with racing insignias, stripes, numbers, and sponsors bring speed to the art project. Ask students to start their engines, blow the whistle, and their pencil cars can demonstrate line racing around a circular table.

Use a brush taped to a baton to demonstrate painting as conducting an orchestra. This inspires another bold act: use a baton with two markers attached at opposite ends to twirl and draw while leading a pretend marching band.

Painting and Drawing Action with Non-Art Tools

Put away school supply boxes and look for old-style luncheonette plastic packs of assorted action figures, farm animals, or emergency vehicles to make art. Switching art tool containers of brushes for pocket toys—erasers, small balls, pencil toppers, or fast food prizes—makes playful and innovative art moves possible.

Fly swatters, sports racquets, or Hot Wheels cars can all be held and moved in a variety of ways, making them great art tools. All it takes is dipping them into paint, some glitter, glue, or even colored sand. Painting or drawing with a whisk, funnel, or screwdriver opens up new tool action. Toy ponies and their footprints move across canvases with fresh and playful spirits, unlike any Crayola tool or art brush. Sticks and stones may not actually break your bones, but they will move paints in new ways and promote fresh art-making moves.

A vast new world of playful art making is opened up knowing that anything can be dipped into inks, dragged through stamp pads, or soaked in paints. Dragging chains or fake nails through paint or riding bike tires into color puddles opens the range of playful moves and actions that can be used in making art. Try out nature's brushes, like grass tied together as a brush, or use gardening tools for painting and drawing.

Children are the original action artists, creatively handling balls, jumping jacks, or marbles that can lead the way to brush plays. Substituting environmental finds for art tools allows for an open view of art with unlimited possibilities. The form and shape of brushes, or any art tool, can be altered to suggest new uses and ways of moving. It's not just brushes or glitter—any tool or supply can be configured or outfitted as something exciting to test drive and play with.

Playful Bodies

Playing with different toys and tools can be inspiring, but sometimes, the body makes the best toy to inspire movement. Children can learn to see the different parts of their bodies—their faces, arms, hands, fingers, legs, and feet—as creative tools to communicate their fancies. Their bodies can also become canvases on which to create new art forms.

Making Faces

Children often enjoy spontaneously exploring facial gestures before any available mirror. Following a creative process of trial and error, invention, and testing of audience responses, funny and scary faces that stretch the limits of facial muscles becomes an art. Teachers can turn off the lights and have students hold flashlights over their heads to combine gesture play with shadow play. Instead of documenting the faces with cameras, students can be assigned to a partner to draw the creative expressions. Or students as partners can become the mirrors, replicating the faces their partners make, to see how close they can get to the same look.

Hands and Fingers

The image of thumb twiddling has been used to symbolize boredom, and it gives thumb players a bad name. Great baton artists, however, know how beautiful twirling can be. There is more to thumb play than thumb wrestling, and children can ad-lib a vast number of play moves with the thumb alone. Students in an art class can demonstrate other finger inventions inside containers, on a stage, or from behind a screen. They can create competitions to invent new ways to shake hands or dress up hands with sleek fitting opera gloves or baseball gloves to inspire hand performances. With a little washable marker or some non-toxic paint, students can decorate their hands for hand-puppet shows.

Happy Feet

Coming up with ways to move the feet seems easy: dancing, running, and jumping. However, the feet themselves aren't often thought of as tools or canvases. But like the hands and fingers, they can become the stars of their own performances. Have students design new sock or shoe styles, where the feet become models walking down the runway. Paint the toes like hair, draw a face on the bottom of the foot, and "dress" the ankles to create funny new puppets. Douse feet in paint, and have students practice funny new ways to walk, as they see how different footfalls leave different prints. Turn the toes into fingers and have students hold paintbrushes and tools with their feet to see what new types of drawing they can create.

Trying Things On

My granddaughter Aliza likes to explore closets. She drags out her dad's heavy EMT boots and patiently attempts to get inside. She puts her hands into mom's fancy high heels to feel the incline and shows her acrobatic art of getting into one shoe with two feet trying to stand without falling. Aliza's many performances are a way to test objects and forms.

This need to try things on can continue in the art class as a means of searching for and discovering new body performances. Everything in the room and environment can be viewed as a canvas for the body, as something to try on for body art, whether the item fits the whole body or just one part. The following examples describe body performances where students animated unusual canvases for video recordings.

Wear a happy sock was a performance by a student who brought in a new pair of colorful socks. In a performance, he challenged himself to improvise many ways to put on and pose inside the sock.

Snack bag grab was a performance where a student demonstrated how one could experience being a different popular snack. The young artist described the different sensations of being inside a chip, pretzel, and popcorn bag.

The inside story of old gardening gloves was a show starring the student's glove collection. The puppeteer reached inside the gloves, improvising different techniques of shaping and sculpting each, where each shape elicited a different storyline.

Pillow dance involved the act of unzipping a large sofa cushion and placing one's hands inside. The soft interior foam was moved about for reshuffling the form into unusual shapes. The grand finale included the student putting his head into the pillow and performing with a soft new head.

Tech performance involved a large headphone and finding new ways to wear it, along with descriptions of the new use.

The wrapper in an art class is not necessarily a singer. One student wrapped herself in a large, stapled piece of paper to perform. Another was wrapped in a venetian blind with many moving parts. The artist's body can be used to perform with a variety of skins.

Full body armor showed a student crawling inside different size boxes covered in foil. Foil covered trashcans and laundry baskets were also entered and moved with as a shell and what looked like futuristic toys in motion.

Learning Through the Body

Merely looking at items from a distance does not always fit the way young artists experience art or find new ideas. Children don't just study nature by viewing it; they get themselves into the dirt and mud. It is the difference between watching television and having the opportunity to climb inside an old TV set. Art students in school find it fun and challenging to enter a form with hands, head, or full body—to feel its space, experience the inner sounds, or explore the flexibility of surfaces to be transformed by play and art.

Each body movement can be unique and fresh and teaches students that they always have art tools at their disposal. Keeping bodies and minds moving playfully and inventively keeps the creativity running and counteracts the restrictive bodily discipline students must maintain the rest of the school day.

Dance Performances

Dance is such an important and prevalent form of movement play that it deserves its own section. Engaging the artist in dance through sounds and fantasies liberates artistic moves and spirits and alters routine ways of thinking and moving in space or over a drawing surface. Dance and musical improvisations with tools over make-believe surfaces, such as an ice rink or dance floor, allow a sense of confidence in making art by playful moving and performing. When art tools become dance props, worries about correct techniques and how art is supposed to be made all melt away.

Dance Party

In the manner of her favorite television dance show, before judges and audience, my granddaughter Emilie and her friends take turns performing dance routines. They synchronize dance moves with play figures to the tune of "Farmer in the

Dell" and other hits from Grandpa's vintage children's record collection. The performers had such a good time creating fabulous team dance routines that I invited them to my art class. In the art room, students armed with drawing tools record their impressions of these young performers on large paper "records" cut for the occasion. As the music and dancing flowed on stage, the art flowed into the students' drawings.

Preparing Dance Floors

A good way to encourage dancing is to create a dance floor. Anything from foam packing pieces to drums to portable trampolines can be decorated as performance stages. A variety of stages can promote and suggest different moves. As students consider the different needs their particular dance inspirations require, they become aware of how movement, sound, and scene interact. Children creating ice dances as figure skaters use shiny plastic drop cloths. Sliding and gliding, putting shoes on one's hand and animating them as a tap dancer may require playing over wood flooring samples. To create acrobatic dances, a bouncing stage can be stretched over a trashcan, between tables, or a portable trampoline tested and tuned.

Asking Art Tools to Dance

When art tools from drawing pencils and pens to paintbrushes or found objects are playfully approached and envisioned to be something other than ordinary tools doing ordinary tasks, fresh art possibilities emerge. If a crayon is not just a crayon but also your prospective dancing partner, that crayon takes on a new function; it's held and moved in special ways. Rehearsing as a dancer with crayons strapped to one's shoes or teaching an old marker new hip-hop moves allows for unique handling, playing, and markings to appear.

Moving Canvases

Students can wear canvases by slipping into simplified poncho-styled paper. Then, they can dance down a row of other students who wield brushes, pencils, markers, or other art tools, decorating the dancer's canvas. Pairs of students can dance together to "La Bamba" and draw on each other's canvas until the song ends. Or students can wear their canvas outside, rubbing along flower blossoms, rolling through the grass and dirt, as nature paints the canvas in unexpected colors and with unique designs.

Students can put canvases in unusual places to dance around and mark with tools guided by their dance movements. Have them wrap wide tree trunks in a paper roll and twirl around the tree, leaving drawing impressions as they circle the bark. Or have them create a conga train, with each student circling the tree leaving her or his design marks. Cover the floor with different canvases—old carpet pieces, butcher paper, leftover tiles, or AstroTurf. Have them dance barefoot and blindfolded while describing what they dance on, or have them interpret the tactile differences in their dance movements, trying to imagine the best type of dancing for the chosen surface.

6

THEMES OF ART PLAY

FIGURE 6.0 A brochure of dream recipes used to concoct a Happy Birthday play.

This chapter describes children's play themes that can inspire individual art classes. The play themes described should be an essential part of home and school art for all grades. They are "guaranteed" to withstand wear or change, and they are all subject to improvement by being stretched and altered by anyone willing to try them in original ways. All plays were tested, and indeed discovered, by children. Using thematic play as starting points allows teachers and students to transcend the traditional boundaries of art making and produce an entirely new range of art that questions what art is or could be.

Birthday Play

There are few things more enjoyable for children than birthday parties. Whether the party is an actual birthday celebration or just pretend, children apply vast imagination to planning the perfect birthday party. It's their passion and art. Birthday play happens year around and involves dressing dolls for a party, plans for table settings, and creating artful solutions to wrapping presents. Masters of culinary sculpting, birthday artists break new grounds in cake creations assembled from hatboxes, erasers, pencil shavings, and shaving cream, among other ingredients. A birthday theme may be celebrated with such fanfare as fantastic light-stick shows that illuminate giant balloon performers. From small affairs played out with party hats and fast food figures, children work their way up to large complex parties for themselves or their pets.

In setting up birthday events, children learn to see in their surroundings a multitude of unconventional home canvases that can be designed and decorated. Birthday innovators earn their stripes and rehearse creative planning skills by playing in the kitchen, setting tables, and constantly redecorating and reorganizing their room. Birthday creations emerge from the practice of making art from home chores and evolve into the works of self-motivated artists with a

FIGURE 6.1 Plays define children's design interests and build art résumés.

mission to create memorable events. The possible themes for birthday party play are wide open, unbeholden to conventions, encouraging planners to dream freely.

Bringing the Party into the Classroom

Can school art be based on joy and celebrating? Of course! Saying to students, "Let's play birthday!" is a call to fun creative time. Recreating happy moments is an important theme in children's art. Large white tablecloths painted with birthday images can be draped over school tables or act as a canopy over illustrated placemats and utensils constructed from wires and sticks. Freshly dipped foam shapes can be served up as ice cream desserts with flowing paint colors settling over white paper plates. Students can work in teams to compete for the best cake artist title.

Birthdays, Play, and Making Art

The birthday art children create in fantasy play is a notch above their actual parties. In the real world, parents plan most children's birthdays. Most are assembly line parties, held expediently away from home in "party palaces" that function like a convenience store. There is a little skating, a little bowling, tokens for video games, and tickets to stock prizes. Mechanized puppet shows play while children eat fast food. To personalize the event, parents pick up a kit of matching plates, cups, and napkins representing the current Disney film or popular cartoon character. In such a hurried world, there is no time to cater to children's fantasies. At a mass-market party place, even the child's name may be misspelled on the cake. No wonder when children come home with candy, prizes, and presents, they use them to set up the spectacular birthday events they envision. Disappointment is a driving force for this important play theme to blossom in the art class.

That's why these days the best parties are in the art room. After many birthdays in party palaces, children now find the art room to be the preferred site to stage a party. Here students can custom design every detail of an event and showcase imaginative birthday ideas. Realizing how much everyone loves birthdays, the designation of the art room as a fabulous catering hall can be applied with pride, bearing photos of past events from a glorious history.

Ultimate Birthday Plans

Voicing and sketching innovative plans and concepts should become an important activity in an art class. This can include any kind of pretend party or event planning. Dreaming of birthdays can be as much fun as constructing them, and many of children's best birthday art ideas begin as just that: a dream, a vision, that can be shared with the class. This is their version of conceptual art—a media form in which children excel. One child describes a party where a large, stuffed giraffe is an honored guest and everything for the party is to be made from Legos. They provide details for everything from an extreme cake to the party favors in great detail. Listening to young birthday planners' spirited ideas is being an audience to great verbal art. If parents and art teachers close their eyes, they can partake in children's visions described in fantastic terms. An actively interested audience helps to fill in the details of building birthday dreams.

The Cake Boss

Children of all ages like the television food show *Cake Boss*. Putting on aprons and chef hats, they can pretend to be in charge of their own cake making. Birthday cake fantasies spark imaginative artistry that can flow with colors and paints or build the finest towers. On cake plates and stands, Cake Bosses shape stacks of sponges or giftwrapped boxes with painted foam insets of delicious-looking fillings. Plating for a party is children's high art. Served with a painted spoon, plastic see-through cake slices—with gummy worm and colored rubber band fillings, topped with flowers made from hair bows—show off a young chef's creation.

In the art class, sometimes the cake is more than just a party favor. It becomes a scene for adventure and even other fantasy play. Students create roads to drive up cake-mountains, or they create frosted slopes for skiers. Tiny figures can live inside cake fancies or dance around the summit. Students can dress up as cakes or hide inside large containers decorated like a cake. Free access to great finds and living among interesting objects at home and in the art class allows a Cake Boss's eyes and mind to wander and wonder at all of the decorative possibilities.

Birthday Kits to Keep the Party Rolling

Everyone participating in making a fabulous birthday wants to take it home and keep the fantasy going. What's needed for a perpetual birthday kit that can be carried anywhere? First, a carrying case is essential, such as refurbished cake boxes or cake shaped hatboxes to carry the party assembly parts. These cases can be filled with any item that seems party-worthy; there are no rules.

Blank Canvases

Everyone has heard of a white Christmas, but what about a white birthday? White paper tablecloths, placemats, napkins, plates, cups, and utensils become fresh canvases. The students can dress entirely in white, so they can create every color and design every detail of their party.

Decorating Party Places

The door, the art room, the tables, the place settings, prizes, utensils, and goodie bags are just some of the pieces and tools used by art-room party decorators. From decorating individual presents, the table and room are the next big challenge to wrap and decorate. Children playing birthday decorators use everything in the room; signs, hangings, and decorative touches turn birthdays into an early environmentalist approach to art. Friends can become design teams to invent together and decorate every inch of a home or an art room.

The Birthday Sleepover

A pretend sleepover can be a great accompaniment to the party planning, and students can bring their favorite play figure guests. Using whatever is there, the objects and forms within the grasp of creative hands are turned into beds or snack bars—whatever is needed to satisfy an important event. The art room paper trolley is essential, as students fold and staple pillows, sheets, and sleeping bags. Floor plans for games, sculpted stands for the birthday cake ceremony, and a contest exhibit of glow-in-the-dark nails can all be part of the plan. Balloons make great floral arrangements, and artistic menus can be concocted for the morning special breakfast. An amazing birthday sleepover with all its goody bags and details can be envisioned and tested in the art class.

Happy Birthday

It's no surprise that children love birthdays. In what other art theme do they get to be a star, to have people celebrate and to sing just for them? They can pick the cake and eat their favorite foods. At the same time, they get a mountain of presents, surprises wrapped just for them. If it were possible, children would have nonstop birthday parties. Birthdays are a primer for understanding the art children make to celebrate, to have fun, to satisfy themselves and make themselves feel good. Birthday party play is created for the joy of gathering and making things with friends. Art teachers can distill the many ingredients that make up this celebration and author many different kinds of classroom play and artworks on the party theme.

The study of children's birthday parties needs to be a significant part of art teacher education. Learning from the way children rehearse, plan, and create birthdays guides the designs for similar events to take place in an art class. Understanding how children create birthday art helps us appreciate the essence of art teaching: listening, being guided by young artists' home play and creative ideas. Without it, the art classroom becomes like those impersonal party palaces, doling out the same purchased materials and set projects to everyone.

The Inspiration of Birthday Play

Birthday play is for everyone, no matter the age. And the lessons young children learn from this play stay with them as they age. Emilie, now older, sees herself as playing an event designer. She makes up business cards from repainted playing cards, listing her art as party planning. She skillfully sculpts scale models for school events, including miniature cakes and dessert tables. Still motivated by early birthday play, now she creates entire rooms as environments for celebrating. For her, and for all children who learn to embrace play as part of their art, the party never has to stop.

Adventure Play

In the not-so-distant past, just before video games and tech toys, children used to play around the house, creating forts under the kitchen table and leaping across the ocean by jumping from one mattress to another. Children played detectives and spies, creating secret codes, and for safety, crawled into interesting openings in and around the house. Backyards were playgrounds for new adventures and test grounds for secret missions staged in old barns or tool sheds. Vacant lots just called out for adventurers. We used what was around, making up stories about the different places where our adventures took place.

Adventure play feeds the imaginative side of young artists; it engages them in visualizing new places, telling fantastic narratives, and opening dreams of events to be made real. Active play adventures deal with constructing and inhabiting imaginary places that exhilarate children, make them feel fierce with the possibilities of exploration. Today, it is more important than ever, at home and in art classes, to encourage youngsters of all ages to get out of their seats and physically set up imaginary worlds.

We all know the faces of students who are physically in class, yet somewhere else. Adventure plays provide the opportunity to wander off tracks designed by adults and take legitimate flights of imagination, to fantasize doing amazing things. By giving students a safari hat, stamping passports, offering preventative inoculations, and encouraging children to fantasize adventure scripts, the art classroom gives them access to a large world beyond the known. Children can have new experiences and take amazing journeys without actually leaving a room.

Adventure Themes

In my own childhood, during the dark days after WWII, the many plots of destruction became my playground. I found wood and ball bearings to make scooters with sidecars that I used to fight imaginary armies. I found basic tools like chains and wires, canvas and tires to create shelters and to engage friends in secret missions.

When I arrived in America in the late 1950s, our apartment near Brighton Beach, New York, was also adjacent to an adventure playground. The empty beach during the winter was not cared for, and had all the piles of raw materials needed to build adventure crafts to sail the seven seas. It is no wonder that when I became an art teacher, I looked upon my room as an adventure playground and invited children to formulate their own explorations.

The first lesson I taught at P.S. 157, in Brooklyn, I recall bringing a load of supermarket crates and boxes to be linked and aligned. With AAA maps, called Trip Kits, taped to the floor as a drop cloth, an express train departed from the art room inviting students for a fantasy ride. Familiar with the Magic School Bus, everyone was more than willing to climb aboard a vehicle that offered quirky exploits. To encourage the sense of adventure, it helps to start a class journey with reserved tickets for everyone to board. A trip shared by the class demonstrates how the entire classroom provides access to adventure, so students can be inspired to make their own travel plans and adventure sketches. The following vignettes are stories of some of their adventures:

To a recent class, a noble parent arrived, delivering a rolled up oriental carpet on his shoulder. Taped to the carpet were his son's adventure plans. All that was needed was the space to set up a runway for the magic carpet's flight since the adventurous vision came complete with a fan for lift, cotton clouds to greet, and play cameras to record the sites.

Another student wanted to borrow the largest art room play pool. To implement her dreams of space travel, she brought to class foil quilted pillows to create comfort for a circular space station. There were extra pieces of foil and an ingeniously constructed Lego vest for her space suit. With the help of a chorus to count down, her team was soon ready for blast off.

Artists have diverse needs and often bring in surprising objects that are beyond the inventory of most art rooms. So when an old wooden sled showed up in class, it aroused curiosity. In the student's story, there was a hint of buried treasure, a snow covered spot, and a look at an old GPS device. A hand-drawn map, a flashlight, and food rations showed the seriousness of his intent. To pull the sled, four class chairs were tipped and harnessed as robot dogs.

I was puzzled one day when a student came in with segments of a blue shower curtain. What was she planning to do? She had many great ideas and needed a bit of help to hang the pieces. The curtain, she said, will be the ocean, "To be entered by undersea divers searching for unexpected plants and living forms." After creating the sea cove she imagined, her diving gear was built from trash bags, foam, and a metallic backpack.

Childhood fantasies filled with buried treasure, ideas of mysterious islands, fantasies of forts and alien landings, can be performed in homes and backyards and in school. Adventure tales and creative scenarios provide a rich mix of artistic visions formulated as play. Visionary filmmakers, poetic scenario artists, and conceptual builders of environments carry their childhood inspirations from home to supportive art classes, to museums and film studios. Children's art is a media of creative ideas, a willingness to suspend actuality and to construct fantasy concepts.

A Primer for Adventuring

Adventure plays need an open canvas for students to imagine, design, and travel out of their comfort zone to see new worlds. With imagination and a few expressive props, sea hunt, solo submarine rides, or fishing adventures can start under tiled classroom floors. With a star machine projecting over an art room ceiling the heavens are exposed, and decorated branches can stand as tall trees in a classroom forest or jungle. Memorable flights of fantasy can be balloon rides, with balloons tied to chairs assembled as gondolas. Art rooms can be translated to airports for local travel or orbital space launches. On the wings of a bird, constructed from soft pillows, boundless views can be brought close up with binoculars.

Adventures of the Mind

As a youngster, small openings in haystacks in a Hungarian field served as my fort and secret hiding place. I prepared for many missions digging into the hay and carving out compartments to function as emergency lookouts. Today, as an art teacher I help with provisions, like offering a flashlight for a student planning a hayride under a darkened classroom table. There is play, art, and even poetry in imaginary adventures of slaying monsters or setting up an ingenious escape from a deserted island. Adventures often involve solving creative problems, re-envisioning existing spaces, and visualizing extensions to the art room to anywhere.

Inventing adventures is not just for children. It is the subject of many artists and for art classes of all ages. Adventures open imaginations to experience art as more than just a product of specific techniques. Art rooms set up in adventure modes are vehicles for students to use in exploring. An art room can suggest marvelous journeys and sites that can only be reached by playing. In a media age, children are attached to screens in school and at home. By exploring the sky of the art room ceiling, or traveling to the stars in blasting off from the room, art classes are the final roads, runways, and dock, to take off, to take flights of imagination and escape the ordinary and envision better communities and new worlds.

Store Play

Children see work as fun. My granddaughter Emilie loves to accompany me to the post office to watch the clerk in action and to stock up on envelopes and forms for her post office at home. She admires the stampers and makes her own stamps on blank stickers. Her stamper collection comes from flea markets and rivals the stamper-filled carousel of the town postmaster.

Next, we go to the bank, and Emilie doesn't complain. She loves to visit with Marsha the teller, watching her count bills and coins. Since she frequently sets up her own bank branch in her room, she shops for ideas and free supplies, forms, interesting brochures, and lollipops.

After running the errands, we usually stop for a snack at Emilie's favorite cupcake shop. Here she fills up with small spoons, napkins, and picture menus. As we make our shopping rounds, Emilie inspects the cleaners and car wash with an eye for playing store, and we talk about the props and signs needed for store playing in an art class.

Artists find their inspiration in their surroundings. Children start their store involvement by being rolled about in shopping carts, reaching out, and building memorable art views. Leaving the cart, they become closer inspectors of aisles, admiring the sculptural stacking of giant melons and the art of stock clerks building produce pyramids. Children are drawn to the dazzling action of a check-out lane, a mega-visual thoroughfare. Supermarkets are the museums

FIGURE 6.2 Dress-up plays begin the appreciation for the art of fashion.

children regularly attend, leaving enormous impressions to be sorted and processed through store plays. Lessons learned about art and design in stores can be applied to forward-looking art classes. Store playing as a major art should be supported by parents and studied by art teachers.

Selling Stuff

As a young art student, my favorite store existed around my school on the Lower East Side of New York. I often took my lunch with me, and I would browse along the aisles. Each old display case held entertaining articles, painted plaster pies, and space guns. There was nothing real to use or buy; yet, the place was profoundly evocative of my childhood and the pretend foods and toys I used to stock in my store plays. However, as an art student expected to make "serious art," I never considered playing store as an adult.

When I learned about the playful artistry of a not-yet-famous Claes Oldenburg, I didn't fully appreciate the importance of the work of this adult who liked to play store. It was not until I had my own children and watched them play that I began to reconsider their set-ups and object-creations for sale as important and art-worthy enough to bring to the attention of my students. I first brought to school pictures of my children making and selling jewelry: play pendants, bracelets, and play watches made from found objects. I became interested in my children's different store themes and the range of objects they created, or rather invented, for each shop. I loved their improvised store furnishing: using crates, stacks of books, or borrowed bricks from the backyard. Play figures proudly stood as mannequins wearing sculpture-like accessories and draped in fabrics. They made art of wrapping objects or placing them in unusual boxes with pretend windows. The children refurbished play money and recovered old credit cards for use by customers.

What did I find in Oldenburg's store and my children's store play as inspiring, as art, and something valuable to bring to school? Essentially all art became about shopping for supplies and ideas. As I've mentioned in previous sections, artists always go shopping, and children always shop with creative intent that should be recognized as equally artistic. Kids recognize in every store a wonderful mall of curiosities filled with possibilities, and they recreate those possibilities over and over again in different stores they create at home. When children play store in their room, what they're doing is imagining an exciting place to display their unique inventions and ideas. Shopping play turns ordinary rooms at home, or in school, into inspiring places.

Designing Stores

Every child wants to be a storeowner. They draw remarkable stores and are happy to share their plans in class. Others place store dreams in a box, creating elegant interiors for play figures to shop. Offspring of parents who frequent garage sales are influenced to design tabletop markets of their own.

Mobile stores are also popular. Lemonade stands are a timeless hit, and years ago young store players loaded suitcases with their gear to create an art reminiscent of salesmen's sample cases. Today, the growing interest in food trucks has found its way into children's store play, where card tables or toy trucks are converted to vehicles for moveable feasts.

Playing store brings together young artists; they can work together as a design team or take turns selling and shopping. For example, Halloween outings are often followed by candy store play, in which a group of kids create a setting to trade treats in an assemblage of candy forms and wrapper designs made into art. Children design restaurants, creating table settings, foods, menus, and taking turns as chefs and waiters. All the menu items are formulated from non-food objects set up to look like food. Playing store opens art views to considering toys, candy, and found object creations as making art.

Store Play in School

When I first introduced store play into my art teaching, I felt like a pioneer. Everything my students made was for a store, displayed on boxes, or set up on trays or shelves in the art room. Instead of making individual sculptures, students joined to design and make toy stores. We still use a store theme for all grade levels, inventing unusual pencils, rulers, and pencil-toppers for a middle school supply store. On open school nights, art is designed and displayed as stores in the lobby and hallways. Of course, along with the store play, many other neglected arts, such as wrapping paper design, have had a school revival. Innovative shopping bags are collected like paintings by students who exhibit them and create their own models for play stores.

Store play ideas and designs in the art class derive from students spending time in and absorbing and interpreting store culture in daily life. Almost every conceivable store in the community has been recreated in the art class. Stores proudly feature unique logos, shopping bags, and even cart designs. Some of the play stores turn to real establishments in the school that feel like museum gift shops. Store play is not just for little kids. In our current high school gift shop, the most popular items are painted eyeglass cases, rubber band weavings, and watches made from vintage coasters.

Store play leads to many new understandings about art. The objects on display in an art class are not random still life junk to copy. Innovative items are designed and made for pretend store playing and actual school-based gift shops.

Graduates of store playing learn to recognize that everything around has possibilities, and they are browsing and shopping for their store—their art—all the time. When children at home and students of all ages in school can look around any room inside or outdoors and think, "Oh I can use everything," "I can play with this," or "I definitely could use it for my store or my art," then the student has learned a great deal from an art class. They are ready to be an artist. Basic play that starts at home and continues to thrive in art rooms emancipates the creative individual to invent with all objects and subjects.

Building Play

In kindergartens of the past, playing with wood blocks was the highlight of each school day. Before being mesmerized by media, children used to build with everything from Pringles to stacked pillows and remote controls. In today's test-ridden schools, there is no time to "waste" on open-ended building experiments. The education of independent seekers has become a luxury.

Block play is a model for the best in self-initiated learning, a lesson that art classes can preserve. From a box of wood blocks dumped on the floor, there is instant attraction as children just start construction without an assignment.

Vintage wood blocks are particularly useful for inspiring the imaginations of builders because they do not have fastening devices and instructions that govern each move, like many plastic blocks. Each set of weathered old blocks has a distinct weight and feel that elicits designs from every player. Besides sets, a foster

FIGURE 6.3 A child's room is a studio for pretending, and a model for an adventure playground that is the art room.

home for wayward blocks—unique individual pieces from all lineages—is a great stash for an art room.

Art teachers recognize in children's drawings or paintings whether they had preliminary experience with wood blocks. Having played with blocks, children instinctively understand design and the most obscure foundations of the art of geometry. These students create two-dimensional art that's solidly grounded and elegantly structured. Block playing holds the opportunity to play with balance and fight gravity to scale new heights. Children's block play involves construction and destruction—the yin and yang of solid-form poetry.

Teacher Discoveries and Challenges

The study of home block playing provides clues to importing the art to school. As one art teacher observes, "Young children keep blocks close to the floor. But as children grow from crawling to standing, their blocks also take a stance, moving into space." Another viewer testifies, "Children love the music of falling pieces and discovering the positions blocks take in free fall. They knock down wood structures just to clear the canvas." Tracing, lighting, painting, or the use of new media can be used to further expound on block creations.

With blocks, students make fluid adjustments, trying multiple views, easy to alter, edit, or choose from. No erasers are necessary; no need to throw away papers to start a new drawing. In changing block formations there is no fear, only an endless array of possibilities.

Blocks lend themselves to sculptural abstractions but can also be used to explore architecture, city planning, interior designs, or furnishings—or to visualize new forms in transportation. Block playing builds cooperation that is essential in forming adult design teams. Although children are capable of inventing their own play, an art teacher can add challenges, inspiring them to build with an eye for immense heights with stacks that reach the ceiling, or balance block structures over a water bottle or a stack of books, or stabilize a block sculpture in one hand.

Accompaniments for Block Constructions

There are many different tools and objects that can be integrated into block play. For example, to make their block art less temporary, some students ask for tape or glue to hold it all together. Art teachers can spread white paper rolls on the floor prior to block playing, so that the outlines or shadows of structures can be recorded with sponge brush paintings. Stickers and stampers can be a 2D accompaniment to emerging block creation. Yellow helmets with insignias that say, "We Build the New World," can be made for official art class wear that licenses important block constructions.

Provisions of play figures, dinosaurs, and other objects can be added to block worlds to expand fantasy scenes that may be attached to a base for filming and repeated playing. Blocks are a useful accessory to playing store, school, or airport. Pick-up sticks, rulers, paint stirrers, or wood flooring samples extend the possibilities of block artistry. Stacks of CDs and the addition of foam containers or box padding materials can enlarge the scale, reach, and complexity of block dreams. Scrap wood finds, such as frames, crates, or cigar boxes, can lead block players to consider woodworking and permanently glued or nailed constructions.

Advanced Block Playing

New blocks and fresh settings for playing with blocks can be a theme in school art. It's important to continue block play even beyond the use of actual blocks because it deals with real objects that help students find and test ideas and create models of those ideas. Block playing is to think with objects in one's hands, to appreciate the handmade, and to view artistic power as the ability to design and build anything. In an age of computer modeling, block play is a basic human activity to balance media life.

Advanced block playing is seeing building opportunities and exciting construction possibilities in everything: to build with chips and envision new architectural forms or construct with laundry baskets to imagine new sculptures. Block play with bottled water may create new visions for cities. Post-modern building sets can contain all kinds of daily objects, plain and giftwrapped boxes. Advanced builders learn to see everything as a possible block set, from tall detergent boxes at the market, to a drawer of Tupperware in the home. Students in an art class can build and compare their own ideas for block sets made from crumpled cellophane or constructed with paper shopping bags.

Advanced block players can start any art class with their own block finds and find infinite possibilities of what to do. Life-long block players never run out of ideas and possibilities. Students have invented blocks to wear on their head made from vintage hair curlers and modeled Lego vests. They build on grass with a stack of vintage suitcases. They gather school trash containers to assemble a world-class city. They build small-scale pocket-find constructions with candy blocks and eraser towers. They dream big, inspired by the supermarket to model skyscrapers shaped from bananas.

A giant box of wood blocks, Legos, and all other imaginative objects used as blocks are a necessary supply that can start an art class. Starting with block play on the floor signals to students that the art room is a play site. Different from other classes, the art class starts with active play investigations and student discoveries. Block play preserves artistic confidence and demonstrates how everyone is able to harvest an abundance of creative ideas.

Parents and teachers are key to extending block play by always looking for opportunities for young artists to assemble and build with everything. A case of yogurt can be leased for playful stacking and assembly before the containers go into the refrigerator. Every young artist is a potential builder, an inventor, a designer, and they need to know they are free to play with any object in a lab, test kitchen, construction site, and other such names used for home and school.

Putting Blocks Away

Frank Lloyd Wright claimed that wood block playing was exploring the geometry of truth, an experience in harmony and unity. Wood blocks are like the atoms of art: simple forms that can be assembled to visualize larger declarations. Structuring and organizing blocks is the basis for discovering one's own sense of design, experiencing the act of being an artist, and rehearsing explorations in all art media. Block playing is important for all ages and all grades. Emilie, at age 11, plays Minecraft on the computer. Her deep roots as the official tester of grandpa's many antique store block purchases, before they moved to schoolrooms, places her in champion ranks of Minecrafters. For many who have not played with blocks, the art class can provide important remedial opportunities that will help them become master builders, designers, and inventors later on.

Playing With Art

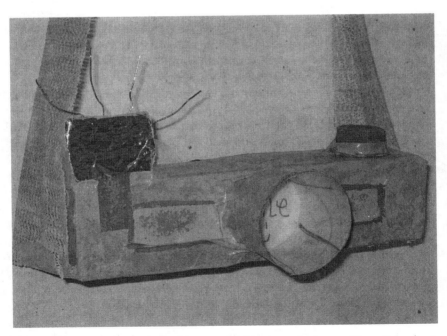

FIGURE 6.4 An art class is for making special things to take home. These items keep on playing and extending creative explorations in school.

The assumption that only adults really recognize, understand, and appreciate art and discuss the "big" issues of art is flawed. Students have wonderful ideas about art and play that tackle this serious philosophical subject in less foreboding ways. Respect for students' ideas as they begin to talk about and engage with art contributes to artistic confidence that their opinions and abilities count. But is there time in school to ask, listen to, take note of, and facilitate the wisdom of students? Time must be made because our students as contemporary artists not only have to be able to make the art of the future but understand how and why it works or be able to respond to doubting audiences that are not always kind or receptive. There are plenty of naysayers, and art education must aid students in sustaining themselves in a world where art is not understood or valued.

Conversations with Artists

A Charlie Rose-style moderator sits around a roundtable with a panel before toy microphones. The art room television show is called *Conversations with Artists*. Simple props like applause signs and stage lights add reality and fun to the activity. In preparation for a weekly show recorded in back of the art class, students contribute cue cards for the alternating moderators. A recording of fourth graders discussing the question "What is art?" offers the following questions and responses:

> "Art is anything I can make with my hands."
> "Art is anything the artist wants it to be."
> "Art is play; art is fun."
> "What is not art?"

As the conversation continues, the focus diverges to other related questions about art.

> Does art have limits? What are they?
> Does art need to be understood by everyone?
> What is beautiful?
> What is original?
> What is a reproduction?
> What is difficult to understand about modern art?
> What is abstract art?
> Does art have to be about something?

Cue cards lead the moderator to ask:

> Can anyone make art?
> Is children's art really art?

Can art be found?

Can an object that is bought in a store be art?

What can be learned from art?

Does the meaning of art come from the artist, or the person looking at the art?

After a *Conversation with Artists*, the video of the show is replayed for the class for additional reflection. Quotes from the show become art and are used in painting banners for the classroom and school hallways for everyone to contemplate.

"Art helps to share ideas."

"We make art to express ideas and use our imagination."

"I can live without art, but I would have pictures in my head that I could not get out."

"Without art the world would be grey and boring."

Playing back the video and letting students see themselves before the class on the big screen lends an aura of expertise to their answers that they generally don't get the chance to enjoy in school. Enlarging the occasion by turning videotaped discussions, artist interviews, and press conferences into public screenings makes for some memorable occasions.

In another play format, the art teacher and students in a seventh grade meet at a pretend café to discuss art. The art class examines photos of famous cafés where artists met to talk, and they use the pictures to change the setting of class furnishings. They have mid-morning tea with play tea sets while conducting conversations.

"Why do we create art?"

"To make a personal world of our own."

"It is comfortable to live in one's own creations in a painting, or in a room one designs."

"To make art is to make a world that is yours, and yours alone."

Not all conversations have to be spoken aloud. One class created handmade bumper stickers that illustrated responses to the question, "Can art be ugly?"

Everyone's art is special in its own way.

Art can be ugly if the artist wants it to be.

What one person thinks is ugly may be beautiful to another.

Thinking about art, and following art-making sessions with thoughtful conversations, is an important part of art classes. These sessions can be set up as creative play acts that disclose and shape life-long views of art.

Playing Museum

The creation of a museum provides many opportunities to appreciate what considerations go into housing the great art of our time. In one class, students reorganize their desks to turn them into an art museum. With desks and chairs upside-down, draped, or stacked, a monumental contemporary structure takes shape. In developing these museums, students must create sketches, models, and proposals for every aspect, including designing the entrance, the lighting of art, storage, and the nature of the opening exhibit, as well as finding and displaying art and even planning the parking area outside. Experiencing the scores of questions, problems, and details posed in design and building stages places students on the front line of making decisions about their museum and helps them understand how art is dealt with in public spaces. This gets them asking all kinds of questions about art and museums, and the interests and comfort of visitors all become a lively debate as students play many roles as designers, staff members, invited artists, and members of the public. With children playing architects, artists, and impresarios, a large art world unfolds from a humble school table.

Playing with Art in a Museum

With imaginary brushes hidden in pockets, students visit the art museum. Inspired by the art on the wall, they pretend to paint using body moves and gestures, dances, and pantomime. Museum play allows for close observation and students creating their own version of the reality in the galleries. With small props and lots of imagination, students enter and travel around and through artworks. Piloting a fly on the wall like a plane, following a crawling bug, or using fingers as viewers and binoculars are some of the many playful ways to enter and get involved with the art on view.

One student steps up to a painting and pretends to be its maker. Students can make up descriptions and stories about the art while they pretend to be the artist, a docent, or a gallery guard. They can put on various spectator roles, too, describing the art as an infant viewer or explaining it to a visually disabled visitor. All of these possibilities can inspire discussions about art from diverse viewpoints. With plenty of roles to go around, students can show how a collector with large bills of Monopoly money, a reviewer with a press badge, an art forger, or an art thief all have different things on their mind and ways of speaking and responding to art in a museum. Active playing in a museum promotes an interest in future attendance and membership in a circle of art appreciators.

Art Appreciation

As a child I was in charge of fringes, receiving a comb to straighten out the decorative strands of my parents' oriental carpets. Later as caretaker of the vitrine, the glass showcase in the living room, I was trusted to dust precious china and wash the sharp cutting edges of the crystal collection. Holding great art is an unforgettable experience that shapes future appreciators and collectors. Art classes can place students close to amazing collections of vintage toys and other antiques and also give them a chance to connect with these items.

Art classes are about building a love for beautiful things. Playing with stunning objects can start with the art teacher's collections. Games played with vintage Old Maid cards or antique game boards place in students' hands the finest American designs. Each art session in school can provide fine examples of design, folk art, and antiques to play with and promote visions of the larger art world and broad art interests.

Art appreciation can't be instilled in children through lectures as easily as through entrusting great collections to students, whether for play or care or both. Old dolls and their carrying cases or old circus sets are wonderful art from which to form a personal foundation for appreciating many other beautiful things.

Art in the Home

Many homes have collections and displays of art that was made by someone in the family. Quilts, needlepoints, ceramics made by family artists are often a source of pride for young artists and a primary lesson about family history that intersects with art history. Playful assignments can motivate students go on home art treasure hunts, to search attics and basement trunks, look through scrapbooks and albums, and ask questions about art found at home. Finding beautiful old Valentines, post cards, and stamps can come from a careful search and give students something wonderful to share. Family art objects, stories, and artists can be chronicled in the art class, building a proud foundation for the next generation of artists in a family.

Students can also serve as playful curators of their family's art in school shows. A student sharing his grandfather's tobacco baseball card collection talks about printmaking techniques, portrait art as illustrated by the history of trading cards. Students posing as art experts explain the history and processes used to make the art and collections of their relatives. While playfully setting a school table with vintage tablecloths, antique cereal boxes, napkin holders, and salt and pepper shakers, students exemplify their connections to historic folk art, crafts, and illustration—art objects and subjects seldom discussed in school art.

Play as Appreciation

A foreboding place like an art museum can be explored as a playground. A subject like aesthetics can be discussed in play scenarios. Art history and appreciation can begin at home. Play can bring art close and in friendly ways, so that it can invoke study in an art class, pride in being a part of an artistic home, and pleasant memories of an art museum visit.

Pretending in an Art Class

Children's favorite play set-ups allow them to be deeply engrossed in playful actions and the creation of fantasy. When Emilie has her friend Sophia over, Sophia comes prepared with an overnight bag and her illustrated Monster High suitcase with play figures and accessories. Emilie prepares for a night of monster fantasy by setting up her playhouse, all rooms, including the classroom-crazy science lab, the weird food cafeteria, and the bizarre music class. The girls settle in for a night of non-stop pretending. They sit on the floor to act out constantly evolving scenes and scenarios, moved along by odd conversations, shifting staging, and improvised prop making. Emilie and Sophia invent songs, choreograph dances, and provide surprising sound effects to an evening of pretend action that feels like a long opera. Oblivious to calls for bedtime or any other adult inter- ference, the players keep going late into the night, aided by glow sticks and flashlights, mesmerized by their fancies.

Keeping the Fantasies Alive

There are few things more important that an art class can accomplish than preserving the young artist's ability to move into deep make-believe states that nurture pretend playing. Many of the themes I've addressed in previous sections include an element of pretend. Pretending allows for the suspension of rules and limitations, to enter an exploratory frame of mind during the act of playing and making art. Playing moves students in an art class to journeys of the imagination that can take form in any art media.

Art room rules need flexibility to pretend and perform, and when the art teacher starts class proclaiming, "let's make believe," "let's imagine," or "let's pretend," she or he sets the open tone of the class. This openness is also conveyed by letting students out of their seats and by having an art room constantly restocked with objects that promote imagination. Favorite pretend partners, like stuffed toys, need to be welcome art partners in class. Since so much of pretend- ing takes place in the prop department of family drawers and closets, the art rooms needs fabrics, belts, mirrors, and wardrobe items that resemble home treasures.

While most parents religiously attend a child's dance or music recital outside the home, performance art of pretending at home seldom has the same dedi- cated fan base. Here lies the need for art teachers to become supporters of pretend art performances in school and to teach parents to be encouraging at home.

The Creative Work of Pretending

Performance art started as an anti-museum art in the 1960s and took time to become the major art form hosted by mainstream museums today. Improvisation is recognized as a key element in the education of adult performing artists. Comedy clubs like the Improv are lauded as important training grounds for comedians. Jazz clubs are respected places to sit in with the legends and hone musical skills. As the forerunner to these forms of adult performances, childhood pretending is at the heart of a creative practice. Children's performances are mostly unscripted improvisation, the essential ingredient to leaps of invention in all fields. Their improvisation skills using figures, objects, and materials help them unlock their imaginations.

In addition to the improvisational skills, pretending helps students problem solve, to practice making scenes, designs, inventions, and fabrications that will help them realize their fantastic plans. When students improvise play or pretend with friends, they usually have to create temporary constructs to support that play. But figuring out what they need and how to imagine, organize, or build it seems less to them like solving a problem and more like an organic aspect of the play process. Of course they'll need to fashion the world's tallest castle to reimagine the Rapunzel story! Need a chorus line of kittens for a big performance coming up? What will they possibly wear? Even coordinating imaginary play with partners requires some amount of planning to get everyone on the same imaginary page.

Diaries of Pretend Play

The following notes are from a week of playing with Danielle, my 5-year-old granddaughter. The examples shed light on reoccurring themes in children's play that can be imported into an art class to refocus school on children and their turf of make believe.

Let's pretend you are daddy and I am mommy. "This is our house," Danielle says, and with a gesture she outlines a part of the porch. She drapes a small table with a large tablecloth and opens one side as a tent. "This is our bedroom." She puts two large dolls to sleep on a pillow in the "bedroom" and says, "Knock if you want to wake them up."

The play is driven by Danielle's spontaneous creative suggestions. Before this paragraph is completed, I am walking a dog on a leash, a piece of costume jewelry Danielle attached to the neck of a stuffed animal. During our pretend session, drawings in the forms of signs, menus, and invitations for a play restaurant and party are also made. There are food sculptures, and table setting art, and a balance beam built from books, and a yardstick for a doll's gym.

Long after the play concludes, amusing stories and pictures from play sessions live on in my art class. I share my stories, and students are eager to tell stories of their own pretend house play. Pretend play can be alive and well on the art room floor and under tables. Homes can be built from laundry baskets, large fabrics, and scrap wood. They can be furnished with the same spirit of improvising and pretending with materials that Danielle demonstrated. Dolls and teddy bears can be welcome in school, but even curious monkeys are willing to play mom and dad. Pretend plays can always counter school moods and yield fresh student ideas. When painting follows play episodes, students just continue by making the painting their pretend playground.

Let's pretend we are in school. Danielle's first question is "Who do you want to be?" Before there is time to answer, she already casts the parts. "I'll be the teacher," she declares, "and you are the student." Bursting with ideas for the day's lessons, Danielle sets up more students on her bed. Instead of chairs, stuffed animals sit up straight, each placed inside her mom's shoes. Every closet in the house is treated as a prop room, and items are freely borrowed for the occasion. I sit in the first row of students, paying attention to the teacher making little "readers." Class is never boring since Danielle finds infinite variations to the theme. Each occasion of playing school is an opportunity to build school furnishings from unlikely objects and act out new pretend affairs in the classroom.

When school-play tales start an art class, everyone is ready with ideas and cannot wait to get started. It's an ideal state to begin an art class. There are plenty of opportunities to invent and decide on what objects could be put together to make desks or how to design an imaginary SMART Board. There is an abundance of art appreciation opportunities, like looking at antique toy schools, school bus toys, or vintage school lunchboxes. Young designers come up with amazing backpacks and new school supply innovations for their students: the figures they sculpt or friends they bring to school. It is well known that many young children could play school in school all day and still go home to set up for more school playing. Popular plays can keep students interested in pretending way beyond the "legal" age of playing school.

Let's pretend we are having a show. For art teachers, it's important to watch and participate in play to be reminded of the joys of pretending. When Danielle extends her invitation, "Do you want to play with me, Papa?" she already has something in mind. "Let's do a show!" There is no script or contract talks, little preliminary choreography or rehearsal, yet Danielle is already creating tickets to invite the family. She looks for a flashlight and moves her trampoline into the living room, while simultaneously putting on a funny headband. Pretend shows just happen, moves and words are improvised, ballet and juggling occurs, and a doll is showcased eating ice cream: it's a mixed-media show. Spurred on by the smallest bit of applause, an encore is suddenly added to the show. If adults are willing to join in, become audiences and pay attention, the pretending is turned into a performance.

Pretending Is Performing

It took artists centuries to discover that all of life can be performance art. For children, it's all pretending and anything can be a show. Everyday acts and objects can be posed, paraded, offered a voice and action, a part in an art class show. Magic acts, a chorus line of stuffed animals, or a rock show with tennis balls becomes celebrated as performance art.

Pretend performances may use toys as props; often play figures star. Children act as directors, animators, set designers, for small or large casts. Children also pretend by dressing up and becoming the performer. Shows may be staged before a family audience, or like a silent tree in a forest, performed without much fanfare in the child's studio, their room.

Children perform many different fantasy enactments, ranging from simple to elaborate. Sometimes, they don't even use props, and other times, they transform the environment to suit the performance. Performances in an art class may start with familiar children's pretend play themes culled from home. By bringing that pretend play into a public environment, it gains recognition as art and can be recorded on videos or saved in other art media.

Teaching Is Playing

Pretending is a natural form of children's art that can be difficult to make room for in art classes planned by adults, filled with demonstrations of techniques and planned art lessons. As children mine a wealth of creative ideas from pretend plays at home, why should this be abandoned as an art source in school? A way to look at an art class is to ask what space, props, or supplies are needed to set up for pretending. Art teaching is playing with kids and promoting their make-believe performances and ideas.

7

CREATIVE ART TEACHING

FIGURE 7.0 Children's rooms and school art classes can be devoted to staging improvised performances.

This chapter discusses how art teaching can be practiced as a way to foster innovation. It describes how art lessons can be challenging questions, innovative experiences, and independent investigations to view art in open ways. The chapter examines such themes as treating students as artists and players, searching for a contemporary art teaching model, or trying on the play artist's role.

Best Practices for the Play-Based Art Teacher

FIGURE 7.1 A child is inspired by interesting places, and the art room needs to be that shopping site to try on objects and ideas.

In this section, I will provide an overview of brief recommendations for ways the play-based art instructor can create a welcoming environment for young artists—an environment that fosters teacher-student trust as well as student creativity, exploration, and innovation.

Greeting Students

Shaking hands with students entering an art room may be old-fashioned for a generation of fist bumpers. However, meeting students at the classroom door with a friendly smile and warm handshake (or fist bump) issues a warm welcome to the art room. As you greet the students, saying "Welcome to our place" imparts a shared sense of ownership over the space. Encouraging students to play unreservedly in the classroom might push them out of their comfort zones, and it requires relationship building, trust between teacher and students, and an understanding that the art room is unlike other rooms in school. This is why art teachers should make an effort to greet individual students from the beginning of the course.

After the ice is broken, instructors can then greet students by acknowledging them as artists and colleagues. Ask them questions like, "What's new in your art world?" "Did you make something at home to share?" "What sketches or photographs did you bring?" "Did you invent or design something exciting?" "Did you see or find something amazing?" Taking an interest in their work from the start of the class keeps them motivated and assures them they are entering a space where their work and ideas will be valued.

Come Prepared

"Never come to an art class empty handed" should be the art teacher's motto. Bringing things to class—personal art projects, interesting found objects, photos, or pre-prepared stories—is a good way for teachers to demonstrate the importance of connecting the classroom with what happens outside of it. Something as simple as designating a sharing table can encourage and remind students that the classroom is a great marketplace where the teacher and students bring and exchange objects and impressions of the world.

Serving Appetizers

Think of the beginning of each art class as an appetizer for a grand meal, where you provide creative tastes and imaginative set-ups that entice students and foster play. Offer students opportunities to see something new, to try things out and discover how something could be made or performed. The introductory plan is not a "how-to," a finite answer to the question of what to do that day, but rather a question of what could be done—where might the next course go?

Each artist, regardless of age, has to fill in an answer. In this way, the start of a class can provide challenges to imagine, try out, and explore.

Show, Don't Tell

Demonstrating possibilities and creative play for students helps them feel more comfortable and lets them see how expansive the imagination can be. That is why my advice to teachers is, "When you feel a lecture coming on, switch to a show and perform it." An art teacher's performing, instead of lecturing, is a powerful solicitation for students' play-acting. Rather than talking about the ways students might use shopping bags they bring to class, take a bag and make magic with it. Become the bag magician and pull the proverbial rabbit out of the shopping bag. Rehearse the many possibilities you wanted to talk about before your students, turning them visually into a thousand ideas. A master art teacher can play with a bag, a scarf, any object to give students' creative impulses a good jump.

Set Up for Treasure Hunting

As I recommended in the section on shopping in the classroom, a great way to begin an art session is with treasure hunting, where students freely pick up objects they find valuable and interesting. As the teacher, you can invite outside shopping or set up the room as an open marketplace. Invite students to open drawers, closets, and treasure chests and discover beauty in all things.

Prime Time Play

Respect for young artists who eagerly come to an art class with a wealth of ideas can be demonstrated by having them go first. Invited to the "podium" during "prime time," they can take responsibility for getting class going on a creative note. This makes them feel important. Instead of a starting lecture and PowerPoint sideshow, the class may start with a show and tell of student pocket finds or a presentation from their Idea Books.

Show and Tell

Another way to get students excited and involved and to showcase their work and ideas is to have a show-and-tell session regularly. It's not just for kindergarten; it should grow with students from grade to grade. In a show and tell, items can be touched and played with, and new materials and tools can be found. One student who visited "Bounce University" can wear his tee shirt and tell all about it in drawings of inflatable environments he designs and shares with the class. Communicating student visions and ideas, and even some teacher projects, means sharing discoveries and inspirations. Another student shows a scrapbook she made of great action photos of the Winter Olympics in the news. In her telling of the story, she might wonder out loud what it would be like to set up paper ski slopes and shiny plastic skating rinks on which to play the winter games with different art tools. Suddenly, a new class project begins. All in all, the objects and ideas from a show and tell are an important prelude to planning and setting up art room play and making children feel proud to share their ideas.

Get Out

In the art room, we take imaginary journeys through a time machine or flights on a magic carpet. But sometimes, it helps to actually leave the known classroom space on frequent field trips to inspire new perspectives. Brief outings—just to the hallway, the lunchroom, or other sanctioned school areas—refresh players. Starting an art class in the schoolyard, casually picking up just a few things that may be needed, provides an array of new tools and raw materials to players beyond what is usually provided by an art class. A small holiday in nature and away from school allows returning players to be fueled by a mix of fresh air and ideas.

Surprises

Children enjoy surprises. They love to open presents to find the unexpected. Play is the art of creating surprise. For parents and teachers, it is making or doing the unexpected. Expecting a traditional drawing lesson, students are surprised to be asked to take their shoes off. Children of course are eager to remove their shoes and socks and try drawing with utensils between their toes. Students can be surprised when their drawing paper is bigger than they are. It is unexpected to be encouraged to move far from desks and wear their canvas in a drawing lesson. For each surprise offered, students respond with playful and positive behaviors. Asking students as they enter the door what type of donut they will be that day, what galaxy they want to visit, what kind of party they want to plan, will keep them on their toes. Surprises like these help to draw them out and break traditional rules and boundaries of what can be done in an art class.

Employing Outside Skills

Many students participate in different extra-curricular activities these days, from music lessons and dance practice to sports and clubs. Giving them an opportunity to integrate the skills they learn in other activities into their play helps them feel like experts even as it helps them hone those skills. They can use their knowledge of music to create new types of instruments, their dancing routines to choreograph a Barbie chorus line, their baseball practice to invent a new kind of field. Connections to students' after-school interests in soccer or gymnastics brings a wealth of themes and fresh creative actions to school art.

This Is My Life

Wearing her rider's hat and galloping on a wooden stick horse she made as a child, one art teacher begins her day. She recounts stories of personal passions, such as taking care of several horses as a child. The performance style presentation includes riding tales supported by a showcase of ribbons from a lifetime of competitive riding and caring for horses. The personal story also features an appetizing show and tell of a childhood collection of toy horses. Students in the art class cannot wait to respond with their own pet stories and to groom, dress, and showcase stalls and riding academies inspired by the play event.

Students should hear about their art teacher who used to play, still likes to play, and considers playing an important path to his or her art. Autobiographical vignettes, accompanied by documentation such as old photos and memorable objects, leave lasting impressions of the importance of early play acts. Sharing personal stories is an important teaching technique that allows art teachers to recount aspects of their childhood experiences to engage, educate, and even inspire students. It also helps foster student trust and help them get to know you as a creative mentor. When they see that play is part of your creative process, children are more likely to take it seriously as they develop their own processes.

Observing Play

As I've previously emphasized, to learn about children and their creativity, one has only to go to the source, to home studios, and discover the art made without an art teacher. Art and creativity are alive and well in home playing, and art teachers need to know about the experiences and play skills with which children enter school to become art students. In order to build art programs that are familiar and helpful to young artists, it is important to see, take notes, film, and collect samples. Future art teachers may or may not have children of their own to observe and sites may have to be found. One cannot be an art teacher, however, without witnessing the art forms of children, how they create, and without having opportunities to play with them. The stories that follow sample future art teachers' observations of children playing. They reveal two important lessons that are essential to art education and how those lessons are integrated into an art class.

Love of Beautiful Things

A future art teacher describes his observation experience while "sitting on the playground floor with my daughter prospecting for gems. One by one she inspects the pebbles and carefully puts the 'most beautiful' into a tissue." The

FIGURE 7.2 In a play act, any object or artwork can be the star performer.

lesson here is that children have an eye and the time to look for gorgeous things. What is a more important artistic quality to dedicate art classes to than the love for beautiful things? The art class is a place to celebrate an amazing red pepper carefully wrapped and transported from the produce aisle to class or unveil gems found on the playground.

Another teacher writes, "Examining a box of antique marbles and the opportunity to play with them is a memorable art experience. Instead of only studying things in books and computer screens, art is a time to stop school matters to look at an amazing crushed glove found on the street, or parade march a vintage pull toy removed from its original box." Looking at a leaf or examining and playing with old toys are memorable experiences that art classes can make time for. New fruits and fashion every season are beautiful objects to select from and celebrate in the art room.

The art class needs to be the place to stop and smell the proverbial roses during a busy life as a student. The art room can be a store, a site for treasure hunts, or a marketplace where beautiful objects are displayed and traded. It is the everyday museum where stunning forms can be touched and held. We need an art class filled by great colors and forms for show and tell and to foster sharing and appreciation through play, so the classroom experience becomes one that turns teaching into promoting a love for beautiful things. Many of the lessons offered throughout this book link back directly to fostering a love of beautiful things, as well as fostering creative ways to integrate those things into new art-making visions.

Play and Meaningful Art

Another future art teacher reports,

> When my daughter was five, she made an important piece of art that I have hanging in my studio. After taking lessons on a margarine box, she finally received her first 1/16 size violin. Hugging the instrument, she decided to trace it and then gently color it in soft colors. What students should 'get' from an art class is not a bundle of techniques, but recognizing art as something amazing like a friend; something that can be turned to for expressing our deepest feelings and most meaningful experiences.

Children's earliest play practices are perhaps the closest they come to creating art that has personal meaning. Under such themes as playing mommy and daddy or the birthday party, they exercise their imagination in ways that also help them understand their lives. These signature works are practiced and reinvented by children over and over again. The art embodied in play acts is not an exercise in skill or techniques but rather a statement of love and fear: what children deeply care for or are concerned about. Art classes can host events and discuss situations that allow intersections between what is meaningful to the student to be played out as meaningful art.

Meaningful art is not work that someone tells you to do or demonstrates as a recipe. Personal play acts refocus art on the young artist and her or his needs and thus ensure that art becomes part of students' daily experiences, becomes a way they can think through their experiences that they can return to throughout their lives. Here are some examples of different play scenarios that can build on children's real-life experiences.

The game of life: Replaying life events at home and in art rooms is an important motive for and theme of play-based art. Innovation from observation and imitation, replaying what parents and other adults do in their way, can be expressed through a variety of children's performances. The following are examples of multi-media performances of being a "grown up."

New Year's Eve may not be a typical time for art education research, but there is a lot to be learned by moving away from the traditional adult celebration to watch children partying. Here is what a future art teacher reports:

> Happy New Year! During a brief leave from the adult celebration in the living room, I join a more interesting children's party on the floor in the next room. Before the clock strikes, children prepare funny hats by altering

cup holders and gift bags. Glow-sticks are entwined and worn as bracelets and head dressing to light the party. Chatty guests of custom dressed Build-a-Bears and American Girl Dolls exchange small talk, and taste pretend food and drinks laid out for them. Children are masters of party improvisation, cooking and preparing pretend food displays, dressing "friends" and themselves, and making up jokes till the ball—a foil wrapped mirror ball—is cut loose from the ceiling fan.

After midnight, there is no noticeable break in the merriment. At the children's gala, the tone turns to a lower pitch, as the children start to get their "babies" to bed. (Happily it was not them who had to go to sleep.) Comfortable beds are made from pillows arched over wood blocks and fancy beds set up in the glittering shoes shed by adult guests. The dolls are read to and the guests' coats are used as an awning, controlling the light for sleepy time moods.

For the first art class of the New Year, the party moves to the class. Where else can children pretend and take on adult roles, design parties, and view all this pretending as an art form? After playing homage to New Year's Eve, there are birthday parties and invented holidays to celebrate. With an endless supply of party dreams and ideas for table settings, prizes, and games, the art room is the party palace.

Another future art teacher reports on the creativity inspired as young children take advantage of all the treasures being laid out for an upcoming family yard sale:

Everywhere around the house are "yes or maybe piles." A child's bed and table are teeming with trial still lives, a tableau of jewelry, and counter displays of toiletry containers. A wheeled shoe rack is emptied and prepared to roll out like a multistory department store. The Doll Shoppe in a large basket gets special attention.

Play imitates life, and there are plenty of design games involved in preparing a yard sale. Of course, on individually decorated boxes, a parallel yard sale is in progress. Art class yard sales confirm an art form; setting tables, arranging products are home designing that can be played as school art.

Another future art teacher notes children's preferences for power play:

There are many spontaneous games that deal with power. The children like to roar, growl, and pretend to be fierce animals. Sometimes a child unexpectedly takes a stick to bang on tables, chairs and makes the sounds of explosions with his/her mouth. The explosion noise appears to be necessary to show how hard a little girl can kick a soccer ball.

This is a particularly good example of how play lets children work through their experiences and feelings and bring that work into the art process. Since most of the time children feel powerless at home and in school, the fierce plays they invent provide the power. This is an important lesson for the art class where adults seem to have complete control. Letting the students feel powerful for a change is a good way to start an art class.

From this lesson in observation, teachers can then try to develop their own plans to encourage power plays. Instruct students to use a drawing tool, stamper, or brush by using it to hit as hard as they can. Drum on the art room tables or actual drums, having the children experiment with softness, pressure, loudness, and control. Or start an art class by having students beat a carpet with beautiful, vintage carpet beaters with exuberance and a loud noise. Students will accept the challenge eventually, starting with soft slaps and working their way to good solid thwaps!

Room to Learn

The main thing these observation lessons teach us is to give children room: room to find life's beauty, to work through their ideas and life experiences, to express all the aggressive, noisy chaos that the rest of the school day tries to reign in. Play-based art is a form of life game and teachers can make up games that allow a young artist to feel their power, use their own judgment, make decisions, and act independently.

The Classroom and Beyond

Art is a constant process, and artists work full time. For school art to make a serious impression on students, classes need to encourage full-time playing and making things, so children learn that everything is to be continued. This notion can be conveyed to students by proper lesson planning and homework consideration. Teachers should think about what can be taken home and how it can be played with and what could be brought with students into class.

From Home to School

Ideas and experiences explored in art classes often start at home, and the best creative sessions continue to flourish after class. That's why it's important for every art teacher to encourage students to nurture their imaginative practices beyond the classroom by establishing home-reporting routines. This is different than encouraging students to bring items and projects to share with the class, which is also important. Rather, the home reporting can be focused more on sharing ideas or evidence of more elaborate art projects that can't easily be brought into the classroom. Some teachers may require students to use journals, sketchbooks, idea books, photos, or scrapbooks to share ideas with the class. For more technologically minded teachers and classes, have students create blogs,

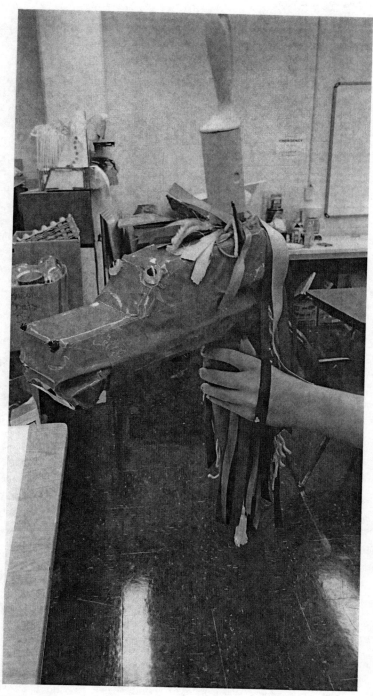

FIGURE 7.3 Children's art is to race and fly, bounce and ride on, and not just hang on walls.

Tumblr pages, or Instagram accounts on which to capture their processes, experiments, and art endeavors.

And Back Home Again

Taking work and ideas home from class is just as important as bringing them to class, since creative playing at school can engender ideas that will continue after school. Leaving the art class with sketches, to-do lists, and things to ponder makes a full circle of imaginative inspiration. Art class play motivates work beyond the class and students prepare objects to show and things to do in preparation for the next session. For example, in class students create playhouses that need furnishings and figures, toys that need to be set up and refined in home use. Living with an artwork, playing with friends and sharing it with parents, clarifies what else an item made in school still needs. Playing at home with school creations also offers clues to what could be done in the next art class, and it keeps the momentum of the class going in home studios.

Life-Long Artists

An art class is a small portion of a young artist's day and should be viewed as an opportunity to build new interests. Doing art in school is not enough time to investigate any play or art fully or leave a lasting impression of being more than just another school subject. Art lessons, like any educational subject, take hold and gain meaning only when they are made relevant to the student's life. Encourage children to use their imagination throughout the day, and help them make creative play part of their daily processes.

Just Making Things

An essential home sensibility to be advanced by school art is young artists' confidence to use their hands to just make things on their own using any found material or object as an art supply. Items crafted by children are often overlooked as their art. As I've explained, a constant challenge of art teaching is to learn about what artists in class do on their own. Art teachers need to be alert to style, what students bring to school that is worn or can be played with and is not created for framing.

Wearable Art

During the past week, my new tween (11-year-old) granddaughter Emilie carried her plastic divider box with color-sorted tiny rubber bands everywhere. Each day, she wears a new variation of rubber bracelets to school. She selects her piece of jewelry as carefully as any other part of her wardrobe. Good care is taken of Emilie's jewelry box each time I borrow it to take to my art class. Her treasures contain a vast history of items she has made from beads and soda tabs, including original "friendship" bracelets of woven wires and painted strings accented with key chain charms. Each session of looking through Emilie's bracelets unlocks memories and fresh ideas for student inventions that will set new fashion trends for weeks to come.

These examples of small things made to wear represent a larger category of student-made art. School play should include small innovations, making three-dimensional objects and real things with which to play or wear. Parents and art teachers need to share their own bracelet memories and begin to recall the larger category of articles made as children.

Learning from Home Studios

Taking stock of what children keep in home studios and how they decorate with things they've made can offer tips for school art lessons. On the pedestal of Emilie's nightstand is a current show featuring pieces of plastic ceramics. Made from a collection of empty medicine vessels, the pieces are assembled as multi-layered vases with compartments filled with decorative candies and flowers picked from the field. On Emilie's desk graze toy animals as well as assemblages of painted and decorated rocks. Covering her doll bed is a fancy quilt made from an assortment of giftwrap and gift bags.

An art teacher's diary and plan book should reflect a compilation of observations about what children make informally. An art class can be turned into a lively Fair, promoting the homegrown items made without adult suggestions. Art teaching that supports young artists demonstrates the wide range of things made by children as an art room model.

Making Lasting Memories

Students raised by technology appreciate using their hands and seeing ideas built in real space with real materials. In our disposable world, students yearn to make things they can take home to play with that will last. Why not transform the art class into a custom toy company where students can build things? No incorporation is necessary, no rules on how-to, just the uninhibited state of artists making the toys they've always wanted but have yet to be invented.

Children of all ages are fond of the handmade. It's what they make and not what they buy that maintains their creative spirits. Looking at the art room as a place that welcomes all kinds of student designs and fabrications assists young artists to feel satisfied and independent that they can invent and shape any material and form. Children who make their own playhouses, school buses, or backpacks eventually will try increasingly bigger and bolder creative ventures. They flourish under the feeling that they have great ideas, and they can invent and make anything, fueled by creative pride coupled with a confidence that takes artists very far.

Making Muses

Emilie takes a chess lesson and then turns the board upside down to play with the pieces. She caters original events with pretend food arrangements for a feast in honor of the king and queen. Inspired by her play, she wants to be the queen. Emilie cuts and shapes foam and jewels for her royal crown. She finds fabric and lace to style her cape. With a majestic scepter (a vacuum cleaner part covered in foil and beads), Emilie points to the dining room chairs to be used as her throne and castle.

The next day, I go to class ready for crowns and coronations, telling the story of Emilie's play while trying to balance her little crown on my head. In my telling her story, Emilie's art becomes public. An appreciative audience of castle fans empathizes with Emilie's play and making stuff as her art. A brief ceremony, a performance-presentation, can set the stage for students to happily join the cast, parading, posing, and bringing to the art class the many experiences and things made for themselves.

Children Making Art for Themselves

While adults make art to hang or sell, as a political statement or a dialogue with the art world, children's art often takes form in playful acting and in making things for their play or as wearable art. Paul Klee, and many other well-known artists who made amazing toys for their children, understood the basis behind children's art and knew that art classes can be about children making great toys for others or for themselves. Making things in the spirit of children can be the basis for school art.

A handcrafted sculpture/painting hanging from a child's door is an important artwork to support in contrast to a store-bought door tag or a doorknob kit from a craft store. Art classes can tip the balance in importance in favor of what children make and the vast number of things bought to entertain them. Parents and art teachers can together raise children without pressure and constraint, allowing them to follow their impulses without being only subjected to adult notions of beauty and art. When school art encourages students to keep making their own items for play or wear outside of school, it sets a solid path for life-long creators and inventors.

Creative Conversations

Students in a play-based art class contribute not just art but ideas. Fostering an environment where students can talk about play, the imagination, experiences, plans, and possibilities can inspire students and help them understand more about their artist-selves and the values in art and play. Where else if not in the art class

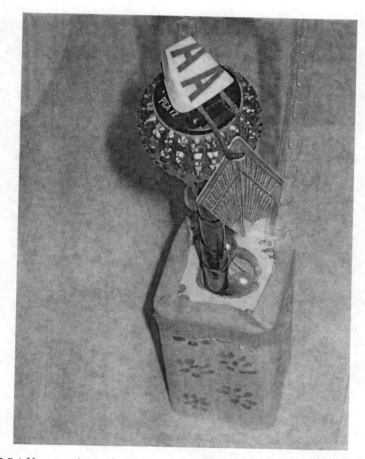

FIGURE 7.4 Young artists make their own things to demonstrate independence, like special drawing instruments with super powers.

can conversations about play be welcome? By asking questions, sharing memories and stories, and even enacting play through speech, art teachers give students permission to reveal thoughts and experiences that often remain unsaid, that are often unsolicited by adults. With a few prompts and plans, art teachers can open the floodgate to students' many play and art memories, get them thinking about art and creativity, and maybe keep them thinking beyond the classroom.

Questions

There are many kinds of questions teachers can ask. They can ask questions to prompt discussions and highlight student ideas, to get students to think and to create enthusiastically, and to give them a taste of what it means to be an artist.

Since playing in the art class already challenges the typical notion of what an art class is and what art is, a good early inquiry to prompt creative conversations would be to simply ask the children, "What is art?" Art teachers benefit from rejecting the idea of "the right answer" and from ignoring the impulse to answer all questions themselves—meaning that they benefit from being open-minded as artists and teachers. In the most humble way, art teachers can proclaim they don't know all the answers about what art is, what it does, and especially what someone else's art should be. They can present themselves as there to learn just as much as the students are, that the class can learn together. Given enough encouragement and freedom, students will provide the most original answers.

Other useful questions for teachers are questions that indicate their support of student exploration and effort. The best of these questions are ones that say to the student, "Show me!" Here's a brief list of possibilities:

"What can you do?"
"What could you do?"
"What are you considering?"
"What are the possibilities?"
"How could that be done?"
"What would be the most unusual?"
"What would be a way someone has never done it before?"

Questions like these help students feel that the art teacher is only interested in what they have to show, say, and plan on doing. Art teaching questions express interest in the young artist's actions and unique thoughts and how these can be realized.

Sometimes, students have questions for the art teacher, questions that the teacher can redirect in order to teach students authority and self-reliance. For example, students often ask, "Is this OK?" "Is this what you want?" Turn those kinds of questions back onto the student: "Do *you* think it's okay?" "What do *you* want?" This refocuses the attention and control onto the student and helps them understand that they can learn to solve their own questions. Instead of being steered by the art teacher's lessons, ideas, and opinions, students will start focusing less on what the teacher wants and more on what they want. Students become used to being the artists in an art class.

In redirecting questions to the students to answer, whether it's about what art is or might be or how it might be accomplished, art teachers also encourage students to begin asking their own questions. This is an important part of being an artist, which often involves talking to oneself and finding answers to self-initiated questions, like the most important question: what should I do? Teaching students to ask this question of themselves can prompt great brainstorming sessions, cooperative projects, or even just give students the opportunity to think of themselves as open to any challenge, any possible answer.

Stories of Play

Previously, I mentioned the importance of adults being willing to share their own play memories and experiences with students. Such moments of sharing not only inspire and excite children, but they can prompt students to recount their own childhood play memories. In art classes we share stories from our lives, validating everyone's creative past. A student recalls covering the sides of her bunk bed, turning it into a sleeping car. Another mentions the creative people from children to adults she played with as a child.

There will always be plenty to talk about as we fondly carry with us the players and playing that shaped our art life. "I used to make clothes for my dolls," a fifth-grader recalls. "I watched mom sew, and she let me use her scraps and pick out buttons." She wonders why and when all this ceased. Another student tells about his favorite monsters, aliens, and dinosaur plays: "I saved White Castle boxes for buildings, and the monsters I was working on would stomp and crush everything." A teenager looks back at her favorite playtime, bedtime, putting dolls to sleep. "I hated to go to sleep and miss something but loved to make play beds, fancy quilts, and sleeping bags for getting my dolls to nap."

It is always fun to remember the coolest places in the neighborhood to look for stuff. Students wonder if they could still go there, and this can lead to discussions of new places to go scavenging. Regardless of age, everyone can engage in lively discussions about favorite play sites at home and outside. Students share their best childhood play inventions. These narratives document the lives of creative artists, while highlighting play as an important art.

Play Talk

Creative conversations also include playful discussions. Ask the students, "Who had chocolate soup for breakfast this morning?" "What did it taste like?" Conversations can go on, discussing ingredients or envisioning choices in unusual toppings. Playful suggestions and requests can also feed inventive actions: "It must be hard to draw with an elephant sitting on your pencil!" "Can you use an egg to paint today? I forgot to buy brushes." "Let's put on multiple goggles and pretend we're flies!" The willingness to be silly and engage in play talk stirs zany and inventive thoughts and motivates play. Silly talk uses humor to engage student imaginations and also emphasizes the unique nature of the art class environment, where silly is good.

Listening

Faith in young artists and their creative abilities can be demonstrated by art teachers who show not only that they can talk to their students as individuals but also listen to them. A teacher's willingness to listen conveys respect and provides a sense of security for students. It demonstrates interest and requires patience, waiting for the students to open up, be playful, and share their objects and visions in public. When students recognize an active and interested listener, they share and help steer the agenda. This is why greeting students at the door, asking them about their projects, and having students share with the class are my recommended best practices—because these moments provide an opportunity to listen.

Listening to what each child is saying and showing validates their feelings and confidence in their ideas. Only by listening to students reflecting on their play and creations can the art teacher really help and provide insightful responses to the many directions a play or work of art can take. Listening makes it easier to leave as many decisions as possible to each player: where to play or what a play may need or involve can be left to students. No steering, leading, directing, interpreting, or suggesting is necessary. Respect for children's ideas and recognition that they are capable of solving their own problems helps students gain artistic self-respect, as the student leads and the art teacher listens and follows.

Playing With Adults

Playing with an adult is an opportunity for young artists to share with someone who seriously engages with their art. Important artist-to-artist conversations, projects, and cooperative play demonstrate to the player that their actions and deeds are a valued pursuit. The art teacher should thus be active and supportive of student creative endeavors, the most important role for co-players.

Adult Co-Players

If an adult is just a director and on-looker, not participant, a play-based art class cannot work. Players join a kind of fraternity, consenting to work together. If adults want to be a part of this, they cannot order creativity or play; they have to get on the floor. For example, one art teacher, showing that holding three teddy bears with two hands is no easy feat, animates these bears to act out a story as narrated by a young artist in the class. This kind of engaging with students as a co-player leads by demonstration, encouraging the students to embrace play readily. As pied pipers of play, adults certify that play is not childish and silly, that it belongs in the art class.

Participation provides a social interaction between adults and children that goes beyond traditional teacher-student roles. The willingness to join makes the art room a lively place and art teaching a memorable play act. With a red clown nose, the adult willing to pose as a mannequin is the art teacher that students dress in colorfully patterned papers and fabrics.

Playing with Artists

Play is the most direct way for one artist (the student) to connect with another artist (the adult) who is a creative individual who can converse using their ingenuity and imagination without taking over. While playing on the floor with my granddaughter, Aliza begins by stacking all the tape rolls she finds into a tall tower. I turn the trashcan upside down as Aliza begins again to build a tower, this time over a high base. She fills the top of her tower with flowers found outside. I bring over the plastic vase as she builds the tallest tower of tapes on a base with a plastic vase on top filled with flowers and licorice sticks. In general, working with Aliza makes plays more sustained and complex than playing alone. Both parents should enjoy equal playtime with their child artists, and school art teachers need to become playmates and step up to advocating play values and demonstrating its wealth of opportunities by joining students in playing.

Adults in Need of Practice

You may think that it's been a while since you've done any serious playing. Many adults can be rusty and uncomfortable making teddy bears perform. To reconnect with the players in themselves, art teachers need to spend time with young players. Teacher education needs to be in the field but not just classrooms. Art teachers on all levels can benefit from visiting home studios, playgrounds, poolside, and childcare centers, to observe and play with kids. Playing together is a unique way of learning all about art from children. If you have not played with children, you cannot be an art teacher. Sharing joyful play moments becomes the highpoint of teacher education, one that makes it easy to maintain a devotion to the profession.

Epilogue

So much of this book is about trust—about learning to trust children's vision, their inner resources, imaginative efforts, and creative explorations. Much of my own creativity was fostered by trust because I was trusted to go out and interact with the world. Our generation grew up on the ground: scavenging fields, digging in dirt filled lots and finding adventures in empty neighborhood places. There, we learned to take chances, be independent, to find things and to be creative.

After school, we were allowed to be outside on our own as long as we came home for dinner. With no questions asked, we came to know all the crevices of our street, first by walking along every inch, then on bikes that allowed us to broaden our explorations around the entire neighborhood. Able to be alone, we could dig and constantly change the topography of the landscape. We collected treasures and made things from trash—old wooden crates and discarded canes turned into toys and furnishings for the clubhouses built. We had much more control over our worlds outside of the house and school.

Today, children are kept close to adults and spend much less time roaming around on their own. "Spend time with your child" is the current parenting mantra. In school, teachers take charge and know what their student does every minute in class. Even older children are walked to school only to enter educational environments managed by adults. After school, students are chauffeured to childcare or more organized and supervised activities with no time to just play and discover alone.

Good parenting for independence and creativity is akin to good art teaching—it involves letting go, allowing children to be on their own, to do things, to experience less supervision and control. Growing up as an artist requires time to wander and be alone, to be trusted to find adventures. Students need the time and place to be themselves—to find things and construct from whatever is around. They benefit from working in an art room where they are not totally supervised, where they are allowed to find things and make decisions about them. Many art teachers report that when they walk out of the room, students do their best investigative work. The art room can provide the creative stimulation that the streets used to provide for earlier generations and prepare children to do amazing things on their own.

The notion that creative time only takes place in supervised activities is not really true. Art teaching does not require holding students' hands at all times, but rather arranging a place where students can be independent shoppers, players, performers, builders, and doers. An art room can be thought of as an exciting place in which to adventure and pretend, discover and make self-assigned work. While it's important to spend time with interesting and interested art teachers, there also needs to be freedom to gather one's own things and ideas. Untied from seats to wander, students play and create imaginary places in an art room. Living in the world as an artist is exciting! One can pick up anything, see possibilities in all things, never be bored, always have plans, and always find things to do. Bringing students together with stuff on the ground and in their environment—through secret spaces, tactile experiences, and imaginative independence—gives them the same opportunities children used to have exploring the neighborhood.

ADDITIONAL RESOURCES ON PLAY, CREATIVITY, AND ART

Select Books on Creativity

Broudy, Harry. *Enlightened Cherishing: An Essay on Aesthetic Education.* Urbana, IL: University of Illinois Press, 1985.

Eisner, Elliot. *The Arts and the Creation of Mind.* New Haven & London: Yale University Press, 2002.

Finn, David. *How to Look at Everything.* New York: Harry N. Abrams, 2000.

Florida, Richard. *The Rise of the Creative Class.* New York: Basic Books, 2002.

Gardner, Howard. *Creating Minds.* New York: Basic Books, 1993.

Jackson, Philip. *John Dewey and the Lessons of Art.* New Haven: Yale University Press, 1998.

Piaget, Jean. *The Language and Thought of the Child.* New York: World Publishing, 1971.

Rogers, Carl. *Freedom to Learn.* Columbus, OH: Charles E. Merrill, 1969.

Szekely, George. *How Children Make Art: Lessons in Creativity from Home to School.* New York/London: Teachers College Press, 2006.

Thiroux, Emily. *The Critical Edge: Thinking and Researching in a Virtual Society.* Upper Saddle River, NJ: Prentice Hall, 1999.

Wagner, Tony. *Creating Innovators: The Making of Young People Who Will Change the World.* New York: Scribner, 2012.

Select Books on Creative Art Teaching

Cottrell, June. *Teaching With Creative Dramatics.* Skokie, IL: National Textbook Company, 1979.

Douglas, K. M. & Jaquith, D. B. *Engaging Learners Through Artmaking: Choice-Based Art Education in the Classroom.* New York: Teachers College Press, 2009.

Einon, Dorothy. *Creative Child: Recognize and Stimulate Your Child's Natural Talent.* London: Octopus Publishing Group, 2002.

Jaquith, D. B. & Hathaway, N. E. (Eds.) *The Learner-Directed Classroom: Developing Creative Thinking Skills Through Art*. New York: Teachers College Press, 2012.

Osborn, Alex. *Applied Imagination: Principles and Procedures of Creative Problem-Solving*. New York: Charles Scribner's Sons, 1973.

Sarason, Seymour B. *Teaching as a Performing Art*. New York/London: Teachers College Press, 2002.

Szekely, George. *Encouraging Creativity in Art Lessons*. New York/London: Teachers College Press, 1988.

Szekely, George. *The Art of Teaching Art*. Upper Saddle River, NJ: Pearson Education, 2007.

Szekely, George. *Art Teaching: From Elementary to Middle School*. New York/London: Routledge, 2011.

Tiampo. M. & Munroe, A. *Gutai: Splendid Playground*. New York: Guggenheim Museum Publications, 2013.

Select Books on Play

Chandler, Barbara. *The Essence of Play: A Child's Occupation*. Bethesda, MD: The American Occupational Therapy Association, 1997.

Hughes, Fergus P. *Children, Play, and Development*. Needham Heights, MA: Allyn & Bacon, 1991.

Kinchin, J. & O'Connor, A. *Century of the Child: Growing by Design 1900–2000*. New York: The Museum of Modern Art, 2012.

Oppenheim, Joanne. *Kids and Play: The Bank Street College of Education Child Development Series*. New York: Ballantine Books, 1984.

Pellegrini, Anthony. *Recess: Its Role in Education and Development*. Mahway, NJ: Lawrence Erlbaum Associates, 1984.

Solomon, Susan. *American Playgrounds*. Lebanon, NH: University Press of New England, 2005.

Szekely, George. *From Play to Art*. Portsmouth, NH: Heinemann, 1991.

Van Hoorn, J., Nourot, P. M., Scales, B., & Alward, K. R. *Play at the Center of the Curriculum* (4th ed.). Upper Saddle River, NJ: Pearson Education, 2007.

Select Articles on Play, Creativity, and Art

Aune, Alison. (2005). Building with colors and shapes: The modernist aesthetic for young children. *Art Education, 58*(1), 25–32.

Bickley-Green, C. & Phillips, P. (2003). Using visual arts and play to solve problems and foster resiliency. *Art Education, 56*(6), 40–45.

Bleiker, Charles A. (1999). The development of self through art: A case for early art education. *Art Education* 52(3), 48–53.

Carpenter, B. Stephen, II. (2004). Learning environments for show and tell. *Art Education,* 57(6), 4–5.

Check, Ed. (2002). Pink scissors. *Art Education, 55*(1), 46–52.

Corcoran, Kerrie. (2011). Enhancing creativity. *Australian Art Education, 34*(1), 30–56.

Freedman, Kerry. (2011). Rethinking creativity: A definition to support contemporary practice. *Art Education, 63*(3), 8–15.

Ganis, V. & Paterson, S. (2011). Imagination in early childhood education. *Australian Art Education,* 34(2), 79–98.

Gude, Olivia. (2010). Planning, creativity, possibility. *Art Education,* 63(2), 31–37.

Guilfoil, Joanne K. (2000). From the ground up: Art in American built environmental education. *Art Education,* 53(1), 6–12.

Harnstra, Folkert. (2010). Self initiated artwork and school art. *International Journal of Art and Design Education,* 29(3), 271–282.

Hathaway, Nan. (2013). Smoke and mirrors: Art teacher as magician. *Art Education,* 66(3), 9–15.

Jaquith, Diane B. (2011). When is creativity? *Art Education,* 64(1), 14–19.

Marshall, Julia. (20120). Thinking outside and on the box: Creativity and inquiry in art practice. *Art Education,* 63(2), 16–23.

Mathews, Miranda. (2008). How we create the conditions for student's freedom of speech within studies in art. *International Journal of Art and Design Education,* 27(2), 12–22.

Milbrandt, Melody. (2011). Creativity: What are we talking about? *Art Education,* 64(1), 8–13.

Nordlund, Carrie. (2013). Waldorf education: Breathing creativity. *Art Education,* 66(2), 13–19.

Pavlou, Victoria. (2002). Understanding young children's potential in art making. *Art Education,* 28(6), 139–150.

Pearse, Harold. (2011). The lost art of pedagogy. *Canadian Review of Art Education: Research Issue,* 38(1), 5–16.

Pitri, Eliza. (2001). The role of artistic play in problem solving. *Art Education,* 54(3), 46–51.

Pitri, Eliza. (2013). Skills and dispositions for creative problem solving during the art making process. *Art Education,* 66(3), 41–46.

Rufo, David. (2012). Building forts and drawing on walls: Fostering student-initiated creativity. *Art Education,* 65(5), 40–47.

Strauch-Nelson, Wendy. (2012). Reuniting art and nature in the life of the child. *Art Education,* 65(3), 33–38.

Sweeny, Robert (Ed.). (2013). Ten ways of making. *Art Education,* 66(2), 4–5.

Szekely, George. (2000). Painting in the year 2000: A classroom video series. *Art Education,* 53(5), 12–18.

Szekely, George. (2002). Art homework. *Art Education,* 55(3), 37–47.

Szekely, George. (2005). Teaching students to become independent artists. *Art Education,* 58(1), 41–51.

Szekely, George. (2006). 30 years of planning: An artist–teacher's visual lesson plan books. *Art Education,* 59(3), 48–53.

Szekely, Ilona. (2011). Art at the airport: An exploration of new art worlds. *Art Education,* 65(4), 33–39.

Tarr, Patricia. (2008). New visions: Art for early childhood. *Art Education,* 61(4), 19–24.

Ulbricht, J. (1999). The art of teaching: Learning from "invisible" teachers. *Art Education,* 52(5), 39–43.

Venable, Bradford B. (2001). Using role-play to teach and learn aesthetics. *Art Education,* 54(1), 47–51.

Vihos, Lisa. (2006). The bathroom as art. *Art Education,* 59(5), 25–32.

Watson, Jack. (2012). We turned your world upside down: Contemporary art practice in the high school classroom and spaces beyond. *Art Education,* 65(1), 33–39.

Select TED Talks

Retrieved from URL: www.ted.com/talks

Play

Brown, Ilan. (2008 November). *Tales of Creativity and Play.*
Brown, Stuart. (2009 March). *Play Is More Than Just Fun.*
Gupta, Arvind. (2011 April). *Turning Trash Into Toys.*
Izquirdo, Isabel. (2011 March). *Evolution's Gift of Play: From Bonobo Apes to Humans.*
Keil, Steve. (2011 June). *A Manifesto for Play, for Bulgaria and Beyond.*
Tulley, Gever. (2007 December). *Five Dangerous Things You Should Let Your Kids Do.*
Zeisel, Eva. (2008 December). *The Playful Search for Beauty.*
Zickermann, Gabe. (2012 November). *How Games Make Kids Smarter.*

Creativity

Bursein, Julie. (2012 November). *Four Lessons in Creativity.*
Kelley, David. (2012 May). *How to Build Your Creative Confidence.*
Libeskind, Daniel. (2009 July). *Seventeen Words of Architectural Inspiration.*
Limb, Charles. (2012 January). *Your Brain on Improv.*
Robinson, Ken. (2006 June). *How Schools Kill Creativity.*
Robinson, Ken. (2010 May). *Bring on the Learning Revolution!*
Svitak, Adora. (2010 April). *What Adults Can Learn from Kids.*

INDEX

CPSIA information can be obtained
at www.ICGtesting.com
Printed in the USA
FFOW01n2005130416
23217FF